Engraved by H. Richter.

ΑΝΑΚΡΕΩΝ

Published January 1.st 1802 by J. & C. Carpenter Old Bond Street

ODES

OF

ANACREON,

TRANSLATED INTO ENGLISH VERSE,

WITH

NOTES.

BY

THOMAS MOORE, ESQ.

OF THE MIDDLE TEMPLE.

IN TWO VOLUMES.

VOL. I. (only)

FOURTH EDITION.

LONDON:

PRINTED FOR J. CARPENTER, OLD BOND STREET.

1804.

THE PRINCE OF WALES.

SIR,

IN allowing me to dedicate this Work to your Royal Highness, you have conferred upon me an honour, which I feel very sensibly; and I have only to regret, that the pages which you have thus distinguished, are not more deserving of such illustrious patronage.

Believe me, SIR,

With every sentiment of respect,

Your Royal Highness's

Very grateful and devoted Servant,

THOMAS MOORE.

ADVERTISEMENT.

Iт may be necessary to mention, that in arranging the Odes, the Translator has adopted the Order of the Vatican MS. For those who wish to refer to the original, he has prefixed an Index, which marks the number of each Ode in Barnes and the other editions.

INDEX.

For the order of the rest, see the Notes.

AN

AN ODE

BY THE TRANSLATOR.

Επι ροδινοις ταπησι,

Τηϊος ποτ' ὁ μελιϛης

Ἱλαρος γελων εκειϊο,

Μεθυων τε και λυριζων·

Αμφι αυτον οι δ' ερωτες

Απαλοι συνεχορευσαν·

Ὁ βελη τα της Κυθηρης

Εποιει, ψυχης οιϛης·

Ὁ δι λευκα πορφυροισι

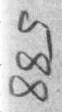

ιϛορωσα

Εσορωσα τας ερωΐας,
Ὑπομειδιωσσας ειπε·
Σοφε, δ᾽ ὡς Ανακρεοῖα
Τον σοφωΐαΐον απαΐων,
Καλευσιν ἁ σοφιςαι,
Τι, γερων, τεον βιον μεν
Τοις ερωσι, τω Λυαιω,
Κ᾽ εκ εμοι κραΐειν εδωκας;
Τι φιλημα της Κυθηρης,
Τι κυπιλλα τω Λυαιε,
Αει γ᾽ ειρυθησας αδων,
Ουκ᾽ εμας νομας διδασκων,
Ουκ εμοι λαχων αωΐον;
Ὁ δε Τηΐος μελιςης
Μηλε δυσχεραινε, φησι,
Ὅτι, θεα, συ γ᾽ αιευ μεν,
Ὁ σοφωΐαΐος απαΐων
Παρα των σοφων καλευμαι·
Φιλεω, πιω, λυριζω,
Μιΐα των καλων γυναικων·

Αφιλης

Αφελως δε τερπνα παιζω,
Ως λυρη γαρ, εμον ητορ
Αναπνει μουσας ερωτας·
Ωδε βιοτην γαληνην
Φιλεων μαλιστα παντων,
Ου σοφος μελωδος ειμι;
Τις σοφωτερος μευ εστι;

REMARKS

ANACREON.

———

THERE is very little known with certainty of the life of Anacreon. Chamæleon Heracleotes *, who wrote upon the subject, has been lost in the general wreck of ancient literature. The editors of the poet have collected the few trifling anecdotes, which are scattered through the extant authors of antiquity, and supplying the deficiency of materials by fictions of their own ima-

---

* He is quoted by Athenæus εν τω περι τε Ανακρεοντος.

gination,

gination, they have arranged, what they call, a life of Anacreon. These specious fabrications are intended to indulge that interest which we naturally feel in the biography of illustrious men; but it is rather a dangerous kind of illusion, as it confounds the limits of history and romance *, and is too often supported by unfaithful citation †.

* The History of Anacreon, by Monsieur Gaçon (le poëte sans fard), is professedly a romance; nor does Mademoiselle Scuderi, from whom he borrowed the idea, pretend to historical veracity in her account of Anacreon and Sappho. These, then, are allowable. But how can Barnes be forgiven, who, with all the confidence of a biographer, traces every wandering of the poet, and settles him in his old age at a country villa near Téos?

† The learned Monsieur Bayle has detected some infidelities of quotation in Le Fevre. See Dictionaire Historique, &c. Madame Dacier is not more accurate than her father: they have almost made Anacreon prime minister to the monarch of Samos.

Our

Our poet was born in the city of Téos, in the delicious region of Ionia, where every thing respired voluptuousness*. The time of his birth appears to have been in the sixth century before Christ†, and he flourished at that remarkable period, when, under the polished tyrants Hipparchus and Polycrates, Athens and Samos were the rival asylums of genius. The name of his father is doubtful, and therefore cannot be very interesting. His family was perhaps illustrious; but those who discover in Plato that he was a

* The Asiatics were as remarkable for genius as for luxury. " Ingenia Asiatica inclyta per gentes fecere Poetæ, Anacreon, inde Mimnermus et Antimachus, &c." Solinus.

† I have not attempted to define the particular Olympiad, but have adopted the idea of Bayle, who says, " Je n'ai poin marqué d' Olympiade; car pour un homme qui a vecu 85 ans, il me semble que l'on ne doit point s'enfermer dans des bornes si étroites."

B 2 descendant

descendant of the monarch Codrus, exhibit, as
usual, more zeal than accuracy *.

'The disposition and talents of Anacreon re-
commended him to the monarch of Samos, and
he was formed to be the friend of such a prince
as Polycrates. Susceptible only to the pleasures,
he felt not the corruptions of the court; and
while Pythagoras fled from the tyrant, Anacreon
was celebrating his praises on the lyre. We
are told too by Maximus Tyrius, that by the influence of his amatory songs he softened the

* This mistake is founded on a false interpretation of a very
obvious passage in Plato's Dialogue on Temperance ; it origin-
ated with Madame Dacier, and has been received implicitly
by many. Gail, a late editor of Anacreon, seems to claim to
himself the merit of detecting this error; but Bayle had ob-
served it before him.

mind

mind of Polycrates into a spirit of benevolence towards his subjects *.

The amours of the poet, and the rivalship of the tyrant†, I shall pass over in silence; and there are few, I presume, who will regret the omission of most of those anecdotes, which the industry of some editors has not only promulged, but discussed. Whatever is repugnant to modesty and virtue is considered, in ethical science, by a supposition very favourable to hu-

---

* Αναχριων Σαμιοις Πολυκρατην ημιρωσι. Maxim. Tyr. § 21. Maximus Tyrius mentions this among other instances of the influence of poetry. If Gail had read Maximus Tyrius, how could he ridicule this idea in Moutonnet, as unauthenticated?

† In the romance of Clelia, the anecdote to which I allude is told of a young girl, with whom Anacreon fell in love while she personated the god Apollo in a mask. But here Mademoiselle Scuderi consulted nature more than truth.

manity,

manity, as impossible; and this amiable persuasion should be much more strongly entertained, where the transgression wars with nature as well as virtue. But why are we not allowed to indulge in the presumption? Why are we officiously reminded that there have been such instances of depravity?

Hipparchus, who now maintained at Athens the power which his father Pisistratus had usurped, was one of those elegant princes who have polished the fetters of their subjects. He was the first, according to Plato, who edited the poems of Homer, and commanded them to be sung by the rhapsodists at the celebration of the Panathenæa. As his court was the galaxy of genius, Anacreon should not be absent. Hipparchus sent a barge for him; the poet embraced
the

the invitation, and the muses and the loves were wafted with him to Athens *.

The manner of Anacreon's death was singular. We are told that in the eighty-fifth year of his age he was choked by a grape-stone†; and however we may smile at their enthusiastic partiality, who pretend that it was a peculiar indulgence of

---

* There is a very interesting French poem founded upon this anecdote, imputed to Desyvetaux, and called "Anacreon Citoyen."

† Fabricius appears not to trust very implicitly in this story. "Uvæ passæ acino tandem suffocatus, si credimus Suidæ in οινοποτης; alii enim hoc mortis genere periisse tradunt Sophoclem." Fabricii Bibliothec. Græc. lib. ii. cap. 15. It must be confessed that Lucian, who tells us that Sophocles was choked by a grape-stone, in the very same treatise mentions the longevity of Anacreon, and yet is silent on the manner of his death. Could he have been ignorant of such a remarkable coincidence, or, knowing, could he have neglected to remark it? See Regnier's introduction to his Anacreon.

Heaven

Heaven which stole him from the world by this
easy and characteristic death, we cannot help
admiring that his fate should be so emblematic
of his disposition. Cælius Calcagninus alludes
to this catastrophe in the following epitaph on
our poet:

* Then, hallow'd Sage, those lips which pour'd along
    The sweetest lapses of the cygnet's song,
        A grape has clos'd for ever!
    Here let the ivy kiss the poet's tomb,
    Here let the rose he lov'd with laurels bloom,
        In bands that ne'er shall sever!

---

* At te, sancte senex, acinus sub tartara misit;
    Cygneæ clausit qui tibi vocis iter.
  Vos, hederæ, tumulum, tumulum vos cingite lauri
    Hoc rosa perpetuo vernet odora loco;
  At vitis procul hinc, procul hinc odiosa facessat,
    Quæ causam diræ protulit, uva, necis,
Creditur ipse minus vitem jam Bacchus amare,
    In vatem tantum quæ fuit ausa nefas.

Cælius Calcagninus has translated or imitated the epigrams
εις την Μυρωνος βων which are given under the name of Anacreon.

                                      But

But far be thou, oh ! far, unholy vine,
By whom the favourite minstrel of the Nine
    Expir'd his rosy breath ;
Thy god himself now blushes to confess,
Unholy vine ! he feels he loves thee less,
    Since poor Anacreon's death !

There can scarcely be imagined a more de-
lightful theme for the warmest speculations of
fancy to wanton upon, than the idea of an intercourse between Anacreon and Sappho.   I could
wish to believe that they were cotemporary : any
thought of an interchange between hearts so
congenial in warmth of passion and delicacy of
genius, gives such play to the imagination, that
the mind loves to indulge in it ; but the vision
dissolves before historical truth ; and Chamæleon and Hermesianax, who are the source of
                                        the

the supposition, are considered as having merely
indulged in a poetical anachronism *.

To infer the moral dispositions of a poet from
the tone of sentiment which pervades his works,
is sometimes a very fallacious analogy : but the
soul of Anacreon speaks so unequivocally through
his odes, that we may consult them as the
faithful mirrors of his heart †.   We find him
there

---

* Barnes is convinced of the synchronism of Anacreon and
Sappho ; but very gratuitously.   In citing his authorities, it
is strange that he neglected the line which Fulvius Ursinus
has quoted, as of Anacreon, among the testimonies to Sappho :

Ειμι λαβων εισαρας Σαπφω παρθενον αδυφωνον.

Fabricius thinks that they might have been cotemporary, but
considers their amour as a tale of imagination.   Vossius rejects
the idea entirely : as also Olaus Borrichius, &c. &c.

† An Italian poet, in some verses on Belleau's translation
of Anacreon, pretends to imagine that our bard did not feel as
he wrote.

Lyæum,

there the elegant voluptuary, diffusing the seductive charm of sentiment over passions and propensities at which rigid morality must frown. His heart, devoted to indolence, seems to think that there is wealth enough in happiness, but seldom happiness enough in

Lyæum, Venerem, Cupidinemque
Senex lusit Anacreon poeta.
Sed quo tempore nec capaciores
Rogabat cyathos, nec inquietis
Urebatur amoribus, sed ipsis
Tantum versibus et jocis amabat,
Nullum præ se habitum gerens amantis.

To Love and Bacchus ever young,
    While sage Anacreon touch'd the lyre,
He neither felt the loves he sung,
    Nor fill'd his bowl to Bacchus higher.
Those flowery days had faded long,
    When youth could act the lover's part;
And passion trembled in his song,
    But never, never, reach'd his heart.

wealth;

-wealth; and the cheerfulness with which he
brightens his old age is interesting and endear-
ing: like his own rose, he is fragrant even in
decay. But the most peculiar feature of his
mind is that love of simplicity, which he attributes to himself so very feelingly, and which
breathes characteristically through all that he
has sung. In truth, if we omit those vices in
our estimate which ethnic religion not only con-
nived at, but consecrated, we shall say that the
diposition of our poet was amiable; his morality was relaxed, but not abandoned; and
Virtue, with her zone loosened, may be an emblem of the character of Anacreon*.

Of

---

* Anacreon's character has been variously coloured. Barnes
lingers on it with enthusiastic admiration, but he is always
extravagant, if not sometimes even profane. Monsieur Baillet,
who is in the opposite extreme, exaggerates too much the
testimonies

Of his person and physiognomy time has preserved such uncertain memorials, that perhaps it were better to leave the pencil to fancy; and few can read the Odes of Anacreon without imagining the form of the animated old bard, crowned with roses, and singing to the lyre; but the head prefixed to this work * has been considered

testimonies which he has consulted; and we cannot surely agree with him when he cites such a compiler as Athenæus, as " un des plus savans critiques de l'antiquité." Jugement des Sçavans, M.CV.

Barnes could not have read the passage to which he refers, when he accuses Le Fevre of having censured our poet's character in a note on Longinus; the note in question is manifest irony, in allusion to some reprehension which Le Fevre had suffered for his Anacreon; and it is evident that praise rather than censure is intimated. See Johannes Vulpius de Utilitate Poëtices, who vindicates our poet's reputation.

* It is taken from the Bibliotheca of Fulvius Ursinus. Bellorius has copied the same head into his Imagines. Johannes Faber, in his description of the coin of Ursinus, mentions another

considered so authentic, that we scarcely could
be justified in the omission of it; and some have
thought that it is by no means deficient in that
benevolent suavity of expression which should
characterize the countenance of such a poet.

After the very enthusiastic eulogiums bestowed
by the ancients and moderns upon the poems of

another head on a very beautiful cornelian, which he sup-
poses was worn in a ring by some admirer of the poet. In the
Iconographia of Canini there is a youthful head of Anacreon
from a Grecian medal, with the letters TEIOΣ around it; on
the reverse there is a Neptune, holding a spear in his right
hand, and a dolphin in the left, with the word TIANΩN,
inscribed, " Volendoci denotare (says Canini) che quelle cit-
tadini la coniassero in honore del suo compatriota poeta."
There is also among the coins of De Wilde one, which, though
it bears no effigy, was probably struck to the memory of
Anacreon. It has the word THIΩN, encircled with an ivy
crown. " At quidni respicit hæc corona Anacreontem, no-
bilem lyricum?" De Wilde.

                                        Anacreon,

Anacreon*, we need not be diffident in expressing our raptures at their beauty, nor hesitate to pronounce them the most polished remains of antiquity†. They are all beauty, all enchantment.

---

* Besides those which are extant, he wrote hymns, elegies, epigrams, &c. Some of the epigrams still exist. Horace alludes to a poem of his upon the rivalry of Circe and Penelope in the affections of Ulysses, lib. i. od. 17. The scholiast upon Nicander cites a fragment from a poem upon sleep by Anacreon, and attributes to him likewise a medicinal treatise. Fulgentius mentions a work of his upon the war between Jupiter and the Titans, and the origin of the consecration of the eagle.

† See Horace, Maximus Tyrius, &c. " His style (says Scaliger) is sweeter than the juice of the Indian reed." Poëtices lib. i. cap. 44. " From the softness of his verses (says Olaus Borrichius) the ancients bestowed on him the epithets sweet, delicate, graceful, &c." Dissertationes Academicæ, de Poetis. Diss. 2. Scaliger again praises him in a pun ; speaking of the μελος, or ode, " Anacreon autem non solum dedit hæc μελη sed etiam in ipsis mella." See the passage of Rapin, quoted by all the editors. I cannot omit citing the following very spirited apostrophe of the author of the Commentary prefixed to the Parma edition : " O vos sub-

2   limes

ment*. He steals us so insensibly along with him, that we sympathize even in his excesses. In his amatory odes there is a delicacy of compliment not to be found in any other ancient poet. Love at that period was rather an unrefined emotion; and the intercourse of the sexes was animated more by passion than sentiment. They knew not those little tendernesses which

limes animæ, vos Apollinis alumni, qui poft unum Alcmanem in totâ Hellade lyricam poesim exsuscitastis, coluistis, amplificastis, quæso vos an ullus unquam fuerit vates qui Teio cantori vel naturæ candore vel metri suavitate palmam præripuerit." See likewise Vincenzo Gravini della Rag. Poetic. libro primo, p. 97. Among the Ritratti del Cavalier Marino, there is one of Anacreon beginning Cingetemi la fronte, &c. &c.

† "We may perceive," says Vossius, "that the iteration of his words conduces very much to the sweetness of his style." Henry Stephen remarks the same beauty in a note on the forty-fourth Ode. This figure of iteration is his most appropriate grace. The modern writers of Juvenilia and Basia have adopted it to an excess which destroys the effect.

form

form the spiritual part of affection; their expression of feeling was therefore rude and unvaried, and the poetry of love deprived of its most captivating graces. Anacreon, however, attained some ideas of this gallantry; and the same delicacy of mind which led him to this refinement, prevented him from yielding to the freedom of language, which has sullied the pages of all the other poets. His descriptions are warm; but the warmth is in the ideas, not the words. He is sportive without being wanton, and ardent without being licentious. His poetic invention is most brilliantly displayed in those allegorical fictions, which so many have endeavoured to imitate, because all have confessed them to be inimitable. Simplicity is the distinguishing feature of these odes, and they interest by their

c   innocence,

innocence, while they fascinate by their beauty;
they are, indeed, the infants of the Muses, and
may be said to lisp in numbers.

I shall not be accused of enthusiastic partiality
by those who have read and felt the original;
but to others I am conscious that this should
not be the language of a translator, whose faint
reflection of these beauties can but little justify
his admiration of them.

In the age of Anacreon music and poetry were
inseparable. These kindred talents were for a
long time associated, and the poet always sung
his own compositions to the lyre. It is probable
that they were not set to any regular air, but
rather a kind of musical recitation, which was
varied

varied according to the fancy and feelings of the moment *. The poems of Anacreon were sung at banquets as late as the time of Aulus Gellius, who tells us that he heard one of the odes performed at a birth-day entertainment †.

The singular beauty of our poet's style, and perhaps the careless facility with which he ap-

* In the Paris edition there are four of the original odes set to music, by Citizens Le Sueur, Gossec, Mehul, and Cherubini —" On chante du Latin et de l'Italien," says Gail, " quelquefois même sans les entendre; qui empêche que nous ne chantions des odes Grecques ?" The chromatic learning of these composers is very unlike what we are told of the simple melody of the ancients; and they have all mistaken the accentuation of the words.

† The Parma commentator is rather careless in referring to this passage of Aulus Gellius (lib. xix. cap. 9). The ode was not sung by the rhetorician Julianus, as he says, but by the minstrels of both sexes, who were introduced at the entertainment.

pears

pears to have trifled, have induced, as I re-
marked, a number of imitations. Some have
succeeded with wonderful felicity, as may be
discerned in the few odes which are attributed to
writers of a later period. But none of his emu-
lators have been so dangerous to his fame as
those Greek ecclesiastics of the early ages, who,
conscious of inferiority to their prototypes, de-
termined on removing the possibility of compa-
rison, and, under a semblance of moral zeal, de-
stroyed the most exquisite treasures of antiquity*. Sappho and Alcæus were among the
victims of this violation; and the sweetest
flowers of Grecian literature fell beneath the

---

* See what Colomesius, in his " Literary Treasures," has
quoted from Alcyonius de Exilio; it may be found in Baxter.
Colomesius, after citing the passage, adds, " Hæc auro con-
tra cara non potui non apponere."

                                        rude

rude hand of ecclesiastical presumption. It is
true they pretended that this sacrifice of genius
was canonized by the interests of religion; but
I have already assigned the most probable mo-
tive *; and if Gregorius Nazianzenus had not
written Anacreontics, we might now perhaps
have the works of the Teian unmutilated, and
be empowered to say exultingly with Horace,

Nec si quid olim lusit Anacreon
Delevit ætas.

---

* We may perceive by the beginning of the first hymn of
Bishop Synesius, that he made Anacreon and Sappho his mo-
dels of composition.

Αγι μοι λιγυια φορμιγξ
Μετα Τηιαν αοιδαν,
Μετα Λεσβιαν τι μολπαν.

Margunius and Damascenus were likewise authors of pious
Anacreontics.

The

The zeal by which these bishops professed to be actuated, gave birth more innocently, indeed, to an absurd species of parody, as repugnant to piety as it is to taste, where the poet of voluptuousness was made a preacher of the gospel, and his muse, like the Venus in armour at Lacedæmon, was arrayed in all the severities of priestly instruction. Such was the " Anacreon Recantatus," by Carolus de Aquino, a Jesuit, published 1701, which consisted of a series of palinodes to the several songs of our poet. Such too was the Christian Anacreon of Patrignanus, another Jesuit *, who preposterously transferred

---

* This, perhaps, is the " Jesuita quidam Græculus" alluded to by Barnes, who has himself composed an Ανακρεων Χριςιανος, as absurd as the rest, but somewhat more skilfully executed.

to

to a most sacred subject all that Anacreon had sung to festivity.

His metre has been very frequently adopted by the modern Latin poets. Scaliger, Taubmannus, Barthius *, and others, have evinced, that it is by no means uncongenial with that language †. The Anacreontics of Scaliger, how-

* I have seen somewhere an account of the MSS. of Barthius, written just after his death, which mentions many more Anacreontics of his than I believe have ever been published.

† Thus too Albertus, a Danish poet :

Fidii tui minister
Gaudebo semper esse.
Gaudebo semper illi
Litare thure mulso ;
Gaudebo semper illum
Laudare pumilillis
Anacreonticillis.

See the Danish Poets collected by Rostgaard.
These pretty littlenesses defy translation. There is a very beautiful Anacreontic by Hugo Grotius. See Lib. i. Farraginis.

ever,

ever, scarcely deserve the name; they are glittering with conceits, and, though often elegant,
are always laboured. The beautiful fictions of
Angerianus *, have preserved more happily than
any, the delicate turn of those allegorical fables,
which, frequently passing through the mediums
of version and imitation, have generally lost their
finest rays in the transmission. Many of the
Italian poets have sported on the subjects, and
in the manner of Anacreon. Bernardo Tasso
first introduced the metre, which was afterwards
polished and enriched by Chabriera and others †.
If we may judge by the references of Degen,
the German language abounds in Anacreontic

* From Angerianus, Prior has taken his most elegant my-
thological subjects.
† See Crescimbeni, Historia della Volg. Poes.

imitations:

imitations: and Hagedorn* is one among many who have assumed him as a model. La Farre, Chaulieu, and the other light poets of France, have professed too to cultivate the muse of Téos; but they have attained all her negligence with little of the grace that embellishes it. In the delicate bard of Schiras† we find the kindred spirit of Anacreon: some of his gazelles, or songs, possess all the character of our poet.

We come now to a retrospect of the editions of Anacreon. To Henry Stephen we are indebted for having first recovered his remains

---

* "L'aimable Hagedorn vaut quelquefois Anacreon." Dorat, Idée de la Poesie Allemande.

† See Toderini on the learning of the Turks, as translated by de Cournard. Prince Cantemir has made the Russians acquainted with Anacreon. See his Life, prefixed to a translation of his Satires, by the Abbé de Guasco.

from

from the obscurity in which they had reposed
for so many ages. He found the 7th ode, as
we are told, on the cover of an old book, and
communicated it to Victorius, who mentions
the circumstance in his " Various Readings."
Stephen was then very young; and this disco-
very was considered by some critics of that day
as a literary imposition *. In 1554, however,
he gave Anacreon to the world †, accompanied

---

* Robertellus, in his work " De Ratione corrigendi," pronounces these verses to be the triflings of some insipid Græcist.

† Ronsard commemorates this event:

> Je vay boire à Henri Etienne
> Qui des enfers nous a rendu,
> Du vieil Anacreon perdu,
> La douce lyre Teïenne.—Ode xv. Book 5.

> I fill the bowl to Stephen's name,
>   Who rescued from the gloom of night
> The Teian bard of festive fame,
>   And brought his living lyre to light.

with

with annotations and a Latin version of the
greater part of the odes. The learned still he-
sitated to receive them as the relics of the Teian
bard, and suspected them to be the fabrication
of some monks of the sixteenth century. This
was an idea from which the classic muse re-
coiled; and the Vatican manuscript, consulted
by Scaliger and Salmasius, confirmed the antiquity of most of the poems. A very inaccurate
copy of this MS. was taken by Isaac Vossius,
and this is the authority which Barnes has followed in his collation; accordingly he misre-
presents almost as often as he quotes; and the
subsequent editors, relying upon him, have
spoken of the manuscript with not less confidence than ignorance. The literary world has
at length been gratified with this curious memo-
rial

rial of the poet, by the industry of the Abbé Spaletti, who, in 1781, published at Rome a fac-simile of the pages of the Vatican manuscript, which contained the odes of Anacreon *.

Monsieur Gail has given a catalogue of all the editions and translations of Anacreon. I find their number to be much greater than I could possibly have had an opportunity of consulting. I shall therefore content myself with enumerating those editions only which I have been able to collect; they are very few, but I believe they are the most important.

---

* This manuscript, which Spaletti thinks as old as the tenth century, was brought from the Palatine into the Vatican library; it is a kind of anthology of Greek epigrams; and in the 676th page of it are found the ημιαμβια συμποσιακα of Anacreon.

The

The edition by Henry Stephen, 1554, at Paris—the Latin version is by Colomesius attributed to John Dorat *.

The old French translations, by Ronsard and Belleau—the former published in 1555, the latter in 1556. It appears that Henry Stephen communicated his manuscript of Anacreon to Ronsard before he published it, by a note of Muretus upon one of the sonnets of that poet †.

The edition by Le Fevre, 1660.

* " Le même (M. Vossius) m'a dit qu'il avoit possedé un Anacreon, ou Scaliger avoit marqué de sa main, qu'Henri Étienne n'étoit pas l'auteur de la version Latine des odes de ce poëte, mais Jean Dorat." Paulus Colomesius, Particularités.

Colomesius, however, seems to have relied too implicitly on Vossius — almost all these Particularités begin with " M. Vossius m'a dit."

† " La fiction de ce sonnet comme l'auteur même m'a dit, est prinse d'une ode d'Anacreon, encore non imprimé, qu'il a depuis traduit συ μεν φιλη χιλιδων."

The

The edition by Madame Dacier, 1681, with a prose translation *.

The edition by Longepierre, 1684, with a translation in verse.

The edition by Baxter, London, 1695.

A French translation by La Fosse, 1704.

" L'Histoire des Odes d'Anacreon," by Monsieur Gaçon; Rotterdam, 1712.

A translation in English verse, by several hands, 1713, in which the odes by Cowley are inserted.

The edition by Barnes; London, 1721.

The edition by Dr. Trapp, 1733, with a Latin version in elegiac metre.

---

* The author of Nouvelles de la Repub. des Lett. praises this translation very liberally. I have always thought it vague and spiritless.

A trans-

A translation in English verse, by John Addison, 1735.

A collection of Italian translations of Anacreon, published at Venice, 1736, consisting of those by Corsini, Regnier *, Salvini, Marchetti, and one by several anonymous authors †.

A translation in English verse, by Fawkes and Doctor Broome, 1760 ‡.

Another, anonymous, 1768.

---

* The notes of Regnier are not inserted in this edition; they must be interesting, as they were for the most part communicated by the ingenious Menage, who, we may perceive, bestowed some research on the subject by a passage in the Menagiana—" C'est aussi lui (M. Bigot) qui s'est donné la peine de conferer des manuscrits en Italie dans le tems que je travaillois sur Anacreon." Menagiana, seconde partie.

† I find in Haym's Notizia de' Libri rari, an Italian translation mentioned, by Cappone in Venice, 1670.

‡ This is the most complete of the English translations.

The

The edition by Spaletti, at Rome, 1781; with the fac-simile of the Vatican MS.

. The edition by Degen, 1786, who published also a German translation of Anacreon, esteemed the best.

A translation in English verse, by Urquhart, 1787.

The edition by Citoyen Gail, at Paris, 7th year, 1799, with a prose translation.

ODES

ODES

OF

ANACREON.

ODE I.

I saw the smiling bard of pleasure,
The minstrel of the Teian measure;
'Twas in a vision of the night,
He beam'd upon my wondering sight;
I heard his voice, and warmly prest
The dear enthusiast to my breast.

His

This ode is the first of the series in the Vatican manuscript,
which attributes it to no other poet than Anacreon. They
who assert that the manuscript imputes it to Basilius, have
been misled by the words Τα αντα βασιλικας in the margin,

His tresses wore a silvery die,

But beauty sparkled in his eye ;

Sparkled in his eyes of fire,

Through the mist of soft desire.

which are merely intended as a title to the following ode.
Whether it be the production of Anacreon or not, it has all
the features of ancient simplicity, and is a beautiful imitation
of the poet's happiest manner.

Sparkled in his eyes of fire,

Through the mist of soft desire.] " How could he know at the
first look (says Baxter) that the poet was φιλαννος ?" there are,
surely many tell-tales of this propensity ; and the following
are the indices, which the physiognomist gives, describing a
disposition perhaps not unlike that of Anacreon : Οφθαλμοι
κλυζομενοι, κυμαινοντις εν αυτοις, εις αφροδισια και ευπαθειαν
εττονηται. οτι δε αδικοι, οτι κακουργοι, οτι φωτεις φαυλης. οτι
αμυτοι. Adamantius. " The eyes that are humid and fluc-
tuating show a propensity to pleasure and love ; they bespeak
too a mind of integrity and beneficence, a generosity of disposition, and a genius for poetry."

Baptista Porta tells us some strange opinions of the ancient
physiognomists on this subject, their reasons for which were
curious, and perhaps not altogether fanciful. Vide Physio-
gnom. Johan. Baptist. Portæ.

His

His lip exhal'd, whene'er he sigh'd,

The fragrance of the racy tide;

And, as with weak and reeling feet,

He came my cordial kiss to meet,

An infant, of the Cyprian band,

Guided him on with tender hand.

Quick from his glowing brows he drew

His braid, of many a wanton hue;

I took the braid of wanton twine,

It breath'd of him and blush'd with wine!

I hung

I took the braid of wanton twine,

It breath'd of him, &c.] Philostratus has the same thought in one of his Ερωτικα, where he speaks of the garland which he had sent to his mistress. Ει δε βυλει τι φιλω χαριζεσθαι, τα λειψανα αντιπεμψον, μηκετι ενεοντα ροδων μονον αλλα και συ. "If thou art inclined to gratify thy lover, send him back the remains of the garland, no longer breathing of roses only, but of thee!" Which pretty conceit is borrowed (as the author of the Observer remarks) in a well-known little song of Ben Jonson's.

" But

I hung it o'er my thoughtless brow,

And ah! I feel its magic now!

I feel that even his garland's touch

Can make the bosom love too much!

> " But thou thereon didst only breathe,
>   " And sent it back to me;
> " Since when it looks and smells, I swear,
>   " Not of itself, but thee!"

And ah! I feel its magic now!] This idea, as Longepierre remarks, is in an epigram of the seventh book of the Anthologia.

Εξοτι μοι πινοντι συνεραυσα Χαρικλω
    Λαθρη ταις ιδιαις αμφιβαλε στεφανυς,
Πυρ ολοον δαπτει με.

While I unconscious quaff'd my wine,
    'T was then thy fingers slyly stole
Upon my brow that wreath of thine,
    Which since has madden'd all my soul!

ODE

ODE II.

GIVE me the harp of epic song,
Which Homer's finger thrill'd along;
But tear away the sanguine string,
For war is not the theme I sing.
Proclaim the laws of festal rite,
I 'm monarch of the board to-night;
And all around shall brim as high,
And quaff the tide as deep as I !
And when the cluster's mellowing dews
Their warm, enchanting balm infuse,

Proclaim the laws of festal rite.] The ancients prescribed
certain laws of drinking at their festivals, for an account of
which see the commentators. Anacreon here acts the sym-
posiarch, or master of the festival. I have translated according
to those, who consider κυπελλα θεσμων as an inversion of
θεσμους κυπελλων.

Our feet shall catch th' elastic bound,
And reel us through the dance's round.
Oh Bacchus! we shall sing to thee,
In wild but sweet ebriety!
And flash around such sparks of thought,.
As Bacchus could alone have taught!
Then give the harp of epic song,
Which Homer's finger thrill'd along;.
But tear away the sanguine string,
For war is not the theme I sing!

ODE

ODE III.

LISTEN to the Muse's lyre,
Master of the pencil's fire !
Sketch'd in painting's bold display,
Many a city first portray ;
Many a city, revelling free,
Warm with loose festivity.
Picture then a rosy train,
Bacchants straying o'er the plain ;
Piping, as they roam along,
Roundelay or shepherd-song.

Monsieur La Fosse has thought proper to length this poem
by considerable interpolations of his own, which he thinks are
indispensably necessary to the completion of the description.

Paint

Paint me next, if painting may
Such a theme as this portray,
All the happy heaven of love,
These elect of Cupid prove.

ODE IV.

Vulcan! hear your glorious task;
I do not from your labours ask
In gorgeous panoply to shine,
For war was ne'er a sport of mine.
No—let me have a silver bowl,
Where I may cradle all my soul:
But let not o'er its simple frame
Your mimic constellations flame;
Nor grave upon the swelling side
Orion, scowling o'er the tide.
I care not for the glitt'ring wane,
Nor yet the weeping sister train.

This is the ode which Aulus Gellius tells us was performed
by minstrels at an entertainment where he was present.

But

But oh! let vines luxuriant roll

Their blushing tendrils round the bowl.

While many a rose-lip'd bacchant maid

Is culling clusters in their shade.

Let sylvant gods, in antic shapes,

Wildly press the gushing grapes;

While many a rose-lip'd bacchant maid, &c.] I have given this according to the Vatican manuscript, in which the ode concludes with the following lines, not inserted accurately in any of the editions:

Ποιησον αμπιλυς μοι
Και βοτρυας κατ' αυτων
Και μαιναδας τρυγωσας,
Ποιει δε ληνον οινυ,
Ληνοϐατας πατωντας,
Τυς σατυρυς γιλωντας,
Και χρυσυς τυς ερωτας,
Και Κυθιρην γιλωσαν,
Ὁμυ καλω Λυαιω,
Ερωτα κ''Αφροδιτη.

And

And flights of loves, in wanton ringlets,
Flit around on golden winglets ;
While Venus, to her mystic bower,
Beckons the rosy vintage-Power.

ODE V.

GRAVE me a cup with brilliant grace,
Deep as the rich and holy vase,
Which on the shrine of Spring reposes,
When shepherds hail that hour of roses.
Grave it with themes of chaste design,
Form'd for a heavenly bowl like mine.
Display not there the barbarous rites,
In which religious zeal delights;
Nor any tale of tragic fate,
Which history trembles to relate!

Degen thinks that this ode is a more modern imitation of the
preceding. There is a poem by Cælius Calcagninus, in the
manner of both, where he gives instructions about the making
of a ring.

Tornabis annulum mihi
Et fabre, et apte, et commode, &c. &c.

No—

No—cull thy fancies from above,
Themes of heav'n and themes of love.
Let Bacchus, Jove's ambrosial boy,
Distil the grape in drops of joy,
And while he smiles at ev'ry tear,
Let warm-ey'd Venus, dancing near,
With spirits of the genial bed,
The dewy herbage deftly tread.
Let Love be there, without his arms,
In timid nakedness of charms;

And

Let Love be there, without his arms, &c.] Thus Sannazaro
in the eclogue of Gallicio nell' Arcadia:

> Vegnan li vaghi Amori
> Senza fiammelle, ò strali,
> Scherzando insieme pargoletti e nudi.

> Fluttering on the busy wing,
>   A train of naked Cupids came,
> Sporting round in harmless ring,
>   Without a dart, without a flame.

And

And all the Graces, link'd with Love,

Blushing through the shadowy grove;

While rosy boys disporting round,

In circlets trip the velvet ground;

But ah ! if there Apollo toys,

I tremble for my rosy boys !

And thus in the Pervigilium Veneris :

Ite nymphæ, posuit arma, feriatus est amor.

Love is disarm'd—ye nymphs, in safety stray,
Your bosoms now may boast a holiday !

But ah ! if there Apollo toys,

I tremble for my rosy boys !] An allusion to the fable, that
Apollo had killed his beloved boy Hyacinth, while playing
with him at quoits. " This (says M. La Fosse) is assuredly
the sense of the text, and it cannot admit of any other."

The Italian translators, to save themselves the trouble of a
note, have taken the liberty of making Anacreon explain this
fable. Thus Salvini, the most literal of any of them:

Ma con lor non giuochi Apollo ;
Che in fiero risco
Col duro disco
A Giacinto fiaccò il collo.

ODE

ODE VI.

As late I sought the spangled bowers,
To cull a wreath of matin flowers,
Where many an early rose was weeping,
I found the urchin Cupid sleeping.

I caught

The Vatican MS. pronounces this beautiful fiction to be the genuine offspring of Anacreon. It has all the features of the parent:

> et facile insciis
> Noscitetur ab omnibus.

The commentators, however, have attributed it to Julian, a royal poet.

Where many an early rose was weeping,
I found the urchin Cupid sleeping.] This idea is prettily imitated in the following epigram by Andreas Naugerius:

> Florentes dum forte vagans mea Hyella per hortos
> Texit odoratis lilia cana rosis,
> Ecce rosas inter latitantem invenit amorem
> Et simul annexis floribus implicuit.

5   Luctatur

I caught the boy, a goblet's tide
Was richly mantling by my side,

                                    I caught

> Luctatur primo, et contra nitentibus alis
>   Indomitus tentat solvere vincta puer,
> Mox ubi lacteolas et dignas matre papillas
>   Vidit et ora ipsos nata movere Deos.
> Impositosque comæ ambrosios ut sentit odores
>   Quosque legit diti messe beatus Arabs ;
> " I (dixit) mea, quære novum tibi mater amorem,
>   " Imperio sedes hæc erit apta meo."

As fair Hyella, through the bloomy grove,
A wreath of many mingled flowrets wove,
Within a rose a sleeping love she found,
And in the twisted wreaths the baby bound.
Awhile he struggled, and impatient tried
To break the rosy bonds the virgin tied ;
But when he saw her bosom's milky swell,
Her features where the eye of Jove might dwell ;
And caught th' ambrosial odours of her hair,
Rich as the breathings of Arabian air ;
" Oh! mother Venus" (said the raptur'd child
By charms, of more than mortal bloom, beguil'd),
" Go, seek another boy, thou 'st lost thine own,
" Hyella's bosom shall be Cupid's throne!"

                                    This

I caught him by his downy wing,,
And whelm'd him in the racy spring.
Oh! then I drank the poison'd bowl,
And Love now nestles in my soul!
Yes, yes, my soul is Cupid's nest,
I feel him fluttering in my breast.

This epigram of Naugerius is imitated by Lodovico Dolce
in a poem, beginning

    Mentre raccoglie hor uno, hor altro fiore
    Vicina a un rio di chiare et lucid' onde,
    Lidia, &c. &c.

ODE VII.

THE women tell me every day
That all my bloom has past away.
" Behold," the pretty wantons cry,
" Behold this mirror with a sigh ;
" The locks upon thy brow are few,
" And, like the rest, they 're withering too !"
Whether decline has thinn'd my hair,
I 'm sure I neither know nor care ;

But

Alberti has imitated this ode in a poem, beginning

Nisa mi dice e Clori
Tirsi, tu se' pur veglio.

Whether decline has thinn'd my hair,
I'm sure I neither know nor care ;] Henry Stephen very justly
remarks the elegant negligence of expression in the original
here :

Eyes

But this I know, and this I feel,

As onward to the tomb I steal,

That still as death approaches nearer,

The joys of life are sweeter, dearer;

And

Eγω δι τας κομας μειν
Ειτ' εισιν, ειτ'. απηλθον
Ουκ' οιδα.

And Longepierre has adduced from Catullus, what he thinks a similar instance of this simplicity of manner:

Ipse quis sit, utrum sit, an non sit, id quoque nescit.

Longepierre was a good critic; but perhaps the line which he has selected is a specimen of a carelessness not very elegant; at the same time I confess, that none of the Latin poets has ever appeared to me so capable of imitating the graces of Anacreon as Catullus, if he had not allowed a depraved imagination to hurry him so often into vulgar licentiousness.

That still as death approaches nearer,

The joys of life are sweeter, dearer;] Pontanus has a very delicate thought upon the subject of old age:

Quid rides, Matrona? senem quid temnis amantem?
Quisquis amat, nullâ est conditione, senex.

Why

And had I but an hour to live,

That little hour to bliss I 'd give !

Why do you scorn my want of youth,
   And with a smile my brow behold ?
Lady dear! believe this truth,
   That he who loves cannot be old.

ODE

ODE VIII.

I CARE not for the idle state
Of Persia's king, the rich, the great!
I envy not the monarch's throne,
Nor wish the treasur'd gold my own.

"The German poet Lessing has imitated this ode. Vol. i.
p. 24." Degen. Gail de Editionibus.

Baxter conjectures that this was written upon the occasion
of our poet's returning the money to Polycrates, according to
the anecdote in Stobæus.

I care not for the idle state

Of Persia's king, &c.] "There is a fragment of Archilo-
chus in Plutarch, ' De tranquillitate animi,' which our poet
has very closely imitated here; it begins,

Ου μοι τα Γυγεω τε πολυχρυσω μελει." Barnes.

In one of the monkish imitators of Anacreon we find the same
thought:

Ψυχην εμην ερωτω,
Τι σοι θελεις γενεσθαι;
Θελεις Γυγεω, τα και τα;

But

But oh ! be mine the rosy braid,

The fervour of my brows to shade ;

Be mine the odours, richly sighing,

Amidst my hoary tresses flying.

To-

Be mine the odours, richly sighing,

Amidst my hoary tresses flying.] In the original, μυροισι καταβρεχειν υπηνην. On account of this idea of perfuming the beard, Cornelius de Pauw pronounces the whole ode to be the spurious production of some lascivious monk, who was nursing his beard with unguents. But he should have known, that this was an ancient eastern custom, which, if we may believe Savary, still exists : " Vous voyez, Monsieur (says this traveller), que l'usage antique de se parfumer la tête et la barbe *, célébré par le prophete Roi, subsiste encore de nos jours." Lettre 12. Savary likewise cites this very ode of Anacreon. Angerianus has not thought the idea inconsistent ; he has introduced it in the following lines :

Hæc mihi cura, rosis et cingere tempora myrto,
 Et curas multo delapidare mero.
Hæc mihi cura, comas et barbam tingere succo
 Assyrio et dulces continuare jocos.

* " Sicut unguentum in capite quod descendit in barbam Aaron. Pseaume 132."

This

To-day I 'll haste to quaff my wine,
As if to-morrow ne'er should shine;
But if to-morrow comes, why then—
I 'll haste to quaff my wine again.
And thus while all our days are bright,
Nor Time has dimm'd their bloomy light,
Let us the festal hours beguile
With mantling cup and cordial smile;
And shed from every bowl of wine
The richest drop on Bacchus' shrine!
For Death may come, with brow unpleasant,
May come, when least we wish him present,
And beckon to the sable shore,
And grimly bid us—drink no more!

> This be my care, to twine the rosy wreath,
>   And drench my sorrows in the ample bowl;
> To let my beard th' Assyrian unguent breathe,
>   And give a loose to levity of soul!

ODE

ODE IX.

I PRAY thee, by the gods above,
Give me the mighty bowl I love,
And let me sing, in wild delight,
" I will—I will be mad to-night !"
Alcmæon once, as legends tell,
Was frenzied by the fiends of hell;
Orestes too, with naked tread,
Frantic pac'd the mountain-head;

'The poet here is in a frenzy of enjoyment, and it is, indeed,
" amabilis insania."

> Furor di poesia,
> Di lascivia, e di vino,
> Triplicato furore,
> Bacco, Apollo, et Amore.
>   Ritratti del Cavalier Marino.

This is, as Scaliger expresses it,
> ——Insanire dulce
> Et sapidum furere furorem.

                                                              And

And why? a murder'd mother's shade
Before their conscious fancy play'd.
But I can ne'er a murderer be,
The grape alone shall bleed by me;
Yet can I rave, in wild delight,
"I will—I will be mad to-night."
The son of Jove, in days of yore,
Imbru'd his hands in youthful gore,
And brandish'd, with a maniac joy,
The quiver of th' expiring boy:
And Ajax, with tremendous shield,
Infuriate scour'd the guiltless field.
But I, whose hands no quiver hold,
No weapon but this flask of gold;
The trophy of whose frantic hours
Is but a scatter'd wreath of flowers;
Yet, yet can sing with wild delight,
"I will—I will be mad to-night!"

ODE X.

TELL me how to punish thee,
For the mischief done to me!
Silly swallow! prating thing,
Shall I clip that wheeling wing?

                        Or,

This ode is addressed to a swallow. I find from Degen and from Gail's index, that the German poet Weisse has imitated it, Scherz. Lieder. lib. ii. carm. 5 ; that Ramler also has imitated it, Lyr. Blumenlese, lib. iv. p. 335 ; and some others. See Gail de Editionibus.

We are referred by Degen to that stupid book, the Epistles of Alciphron, tenth epistle, third book ; where Iophon complains to Erasson of being wakened by the crowing of a cock, from his vision of riches.

Silly swallow! prating thing, &c.] The loquacity of the swallow was proverbialized ; thus Nicostratus:

Ει το συνεχως και πολλα και ταχεως λαλειν
Ην του φρονειν παρασημον, αι χιλιδονες
Ελεγοντ' αν ημων σωφρονεςεραι πολυ.

                               If

Or, as Tereus did of old,

(So the fabled tale is told,)

Shall I tear that tongue away,

Tongue that utter'd such a lay?

How unthinking hast thou been!

Long before the dawn was seen,

When I slumber'd in a dream,

Love was the delicious theme!

Just when I was nearly blest,

Ah! thy matin broke my rest!

> If in prating from morning till night,
>   A sign of our wisdom there be;
> The swallows are wiser by right,
>   For they prattle much faster than we.

Or, as Tereus did of old, &c.] Modern poetry has confirmed the name of Philomel upon the nightingale; but many very respectable ancients assigned this metamorphose to Progne, and made Philomel the swallow, as Anacreon does here.

ODE

ODE XI.

" TELL me, gentle youth, I pray thee,

" What in purchase shall I pay thee

" For this little waxen toy,

" Image of the Paphian boy ?"

Thus I said the other day,

To a youth who pass'd my way :

" Sir," (he answer'd, and the while

Answer'd all in Doric style,)

It is difficult to preserve with any grace the narrative simplicity of this ode, and the humour of the turn with which it
concludes. I feel that the translation must appear very vapid,
if not ludicrous to an English reader.

" Take

" Take it, for a trifle take it ;

" Think not yet that I could make it ;

" Pray, believe it was not I ;

" No—it cost me many a sigh,

" And I can no longer keep

" Little gods, who murder sleep !"

" Here, then, here," (I said with joy,)

" Here is silver for the boy :

" He shall be my bosom guest,

" Idol of my pious breast !"

Little Love ! thou now art mine,

Warm me with that torch of thine ;

Make me feel as I have felt,

Or thy waxen frame shall melt.

And I can no longer keep
Little gods, who murder sleep [] I have not literally rendered the epithet *αυτοριντα*; if it has any meaning here, it is one, perhaps, better omitted.

I must

I must burn in warm desire,

Or thou, my boy, in yonder fire!

I must burn in warm desire,

Or thou, my boy, in yonder fire] Monsieur Longepierre conjectures from this, that, whatever Anacreon might say, he sometimes felt the inconveniences of old age, and here solicits from the power of Love a warmth which he could no longer expect from Nature.

ODE

ODE XII.

THEY tell how Atys, wild with love,
Roams the mount and haunted grove;
Cybele's name he howls around,
The gloomy blast returns the sound!
Oft too by Claros' hallow'd spring,
The votaries of the laurell'd king

Quaff

They tell how Atys, wild with love,
Roams the mount and haunted grove;] There are many contradictory stories of the loves of Cybele and Atys. It is certain that he was mutilated, but whether by his own fury, or her jealousy, is a point which authors are not agreed upon.

Cybele's name he howls around, &c.] I have adopted the accentuation which Elias Andreas gives to Cybele:

In montibus Cybèlen
Magno sonans boatu.

Oft too by Claros' hallow'd spring, &c.] This fountain was in a grove, consecrated to Apollo, and situated between Colophon

and

Quaff the inspiring, magic stream,

And rave in wild, prophetic dream.

But frenzied dreams are not for me,

Great Bacchus is my deity!

Full of mirth, and full of him,

While waves of perfume round me swim;

While flavour'd bowls are full supplied,

And you sit blushing by my side,

I will be mad and raving too—

Mad, my girl! with love for you!

and Lebedos, in Ionia. The god had an oracle there. Scaliger
has thus alluded to it in his Anacreontica:

> Semel ut concitus æstro,
> Veluti qui Clarias aquas
> Ebibere loquaces,
> Quo plus eaunt, plura volunt.

While waves of perfume, &c.] Spaletti has mistaken the
import of κοριθας, as applied to the poet's mistress: " Meâ
fatigatus amicâ." He interprets it in a sense which must want
either delicacy or gallantry.

ODE

ODE XIII.

I will, I will; the conflict 's past,
And I'll consent to love at last.
Cupid has long, with smiling art,
Invited me to yield my heart;
And I have thought that peace of mind
Should not be for a smile resign'd;
And I've repell'd the tender lure,
And hop'd my heart should sleep secure.
But, slighted in his boasted charms,
The angry infant flew to arms;
He slung his quiver's golden frame,
He took his bow, his shafts of flame,
And proudly summon'd me to yield,
Or meet him on the martial field.

And

And what did I unthinking do ?

I took to arms undaunted too ;

                                    Assum'd

And what did I unthinking do ?

I took to arms, undaunted too ;] Longepierre has quoted an epigram from the Anthologia, in which the poet assumes Reason as the armour against Love.

Οπλισμαι προς ερωτα περι ςερνοισι λογισμον,

   Ουδε με νικησει, μονος εων προς ἑνα.

Θνατος δ' αθανατω συνελευσομαι. ην δε βοηθον

   Βαχχον εχη, τι μονος προς δυ' εγω δυναμαι ;

With Reason I cover my breast as a shield,
And fearlessly meet little Love in the field ;
Thus fighting his godship, I 'll ne'er be dismay'd,
But if Bacchus should ever advance to his aid,
Alas ! then, unable to combat the two,
Unfortunate warrior ! what should I do ?

This idea of the irresistibility of Cupid and Bacchus united, is delicately expressed in an Italian poem, which is so very Anacreontic, that I may be pardoned for introducing it. Indeed, it is an imitation of our poet's sixth ode.

     Lavossi Amore in quel vicino fiume
     Ove giuro (Pastor) che bevend 'io
     Bevei le fiamme, anzi l'istesso Dio,
     C'hor con l'humide piume

                         Lascivetto

Assum'd the corslet, shield, and spear,
And, like Pelides, smil'd at fear.
Then (hear it, all you powers above!)
I fought with Love! I fought with Love!

Lascivetto mi scherza al cor intorno.
Ma che sarei s'io lo bevessi un giorno
Bacco, nel tuo liquore?
Sarei, piu che non sono ebro d'Amore.

The urchin of the bow and quiver
Was bathing in a neighbouring river,
Where, as I drank on yester-eve,
(Shepherd-youth! the tale believe,)
'Twas not a cooling, crystal draught,
'Twas liquid flame I madly quaff'd;
For Love was in the rippling tide,
I felt him to my bosom glide.
And now the wily, wanton minion
Plays o'er my heart with restless pinion.
This was a day of fatal star,
But were it not more fatal far,
If, Bacchus, in thy cup of fire,
I found this flutt'ring, young desire?
Then, then indeed my soul should prove,
Much more than ever, drunk with love!

And

And now his arrows all were shed—

And I had just in terrors fled—

When, heaving an indignant sigh,

To see me thus unwounded fly,

And having now no other dart,

He glanc'd himself into my heart!

My heart—alas the luckless day!

Receiv'd the God, and died away.

Farewell, farewell, my faithless shield!

Thy lord at length is forc'd to yield.

Vain, vain, is every outward care,

My foe 's within, and triumphs there.

And having now no other dart,
He glanc'd himself into my heart!] Dryden has parodied this
thought in the following extravagant lines:

————I 'm all o'er Love;
Nay, I am Love, Love shot, and shot so fast,
He shot himself into my breast at last.

ODE

ODE XIV.

Count me, on the summer trees,
Every leaf that courts the breeze;
Count me, on the foamy deep,
Every wave that sinks to sleep;

Then,

The poet, in this catalogue of his mistresses, means nothing more, than, by a lively hyperbole, to tell us, that his heart, un-fettered by any one object, was warm with devotion towards the sex in general. Cowley is indebted to this ode for the hint of his ballad, called " The Chronicle ;" and the learned Monsieur Menage has imitated it in a Greek Anacreontic, which has so much ease and spirit, that the reader may not be displeased at seeing it here:

Προς Βιωτα,
Ει αλσεων τα φυλλα,
Λειμωνιες τε ποιας,
Ει νυκτος αερα παντα,
Παραχτιες τε ψαμμυς,

F 3

Αλος

Then, when you have number'd these
Billowy tides and leafy trees,
Count me all the flames I prove,
All the gentle nymphs I love.

First,

'Αλος τι κυματωδη,
Δυνη, Βιων, αριθμιις,
Και τυς ιμυς ιρωτας
Δυνη Βιων αριθμιιν.
Κορην, γυναικα, Χηραν,
Σμιικρην, Μισην, Μιγιςω,
Λιυκην τι και Μιλαιναν,
Οριιαδας, Νακαιας,
Νηρηϊδας τι πασας
'Ο σος φιλοί φιλησι.
Παντων κορος μιν ιςιν.
Αυτην νιων Ερωτων
Διστοιναν Αφροδιτην,
Χρυσην, καλην, γλυκιιαν,
Ερασμιον, ποθιινην,
Αιι μοννη φιλησαι
Εγωγι μη δοναιμην.

Tell the foliage of the woods,
Tell the billows of the floods,

I

Number

First, of pure Athenian maids
Sporting in their olive shades,
You may reckon just a score,
Nay, I 'll grant you fifteen more,

Number midnight's starry store,
And the sands that crowd the shore ;
Then, my Bion, thou mayst count
Of my loves the vast amount !
I 've been loving, all my days,
Many nymphs, in many ways,
Virgin, widow, maid, and wife—
I 've been doting all my life.
Naiads, Nereids, nymphs of fountains,
Goddesses of groves and mountains,
Fair and sable, great and small,
Yes—I swear I 've lov'd them all !
Every passion soon was over,
I was but the moment's lover ;
Oh! I 'm such a roving elf,
That the Queen of Love herself,
Though she practis'd all her wiles,
Rosy blushes, golden smiles,
All her beauty's proud endeavour
Could not chain my heart for ever !

In the sweet Corinthian grove,

Where the glowing wantons rove,

Chains of beauties may be found,

Chains, by which my heart is bound;

There

Count me, on the summer trees,

Every leaf, &c.] This figure is called, by the rhetoricians, ἀδύνατον, and is very frequently made use of in poetry. The amatory writers have exhausted a world of imagery by it, to express the infinity of kisses, which they require from the lips of their mistresses : in this Catullus led the way.

> —Quam sidera multa, cum tacet nox,
> Furtivos hominum vident amores ;
> Tam te basia multa basiare
> Vesano satis, et super Catullo est :
> Quæ nec pernumerare curiosi
> Possint, nec mala fascinare lingua.   Carm. 7.

> As many stellar eyes of light,
> As through the silent waste of night,
> Gazing upon this world of shade,
> Witness some secret youth and maid,
> Who fair as thou, and fond as I,
> In stolen joys enamour'd lie!

So

There indeed are girls divine,

Dangerous to a soul like mine.

Many bloom in Lesbos' isle;

Many in Ionia smile;

Rhodes

· So many kisses, ere I slumber,
Upon those dew-bright lips I 'll number:
So many vermil, honied kisses,
Envy can never count our blisses.
No tongue shall tell the sum but mine;
No lips shall fascinate, but thine!

In the sweet Corinthian grove,

Where the glowing wantons rove, &c.] Corinth was very famous for the beauty and the number of its courtezans. Venus was the deity principally worshipped by the people, and prostitution in her temple was a meritorious act of religion. Conformable to this was their constant and solemn prayer, that the gods would increase the number of their courtezans. We may perceive, from the application of the verb κορινθιαζειν, in Aristophanes, that the wantonness of the Corinthians became proverbial.

There indeed are girls divine,

Dangerous to a soul like mine !] " With justice has the poet attributed beauty to the women of Greece." Degen.

Monsieur

Rhodes a pretty swarm can boast;
Caria too contains a host.
Sum these all—of brown or fair
You may count two thousand there!
What, you gaze! I pray you, peace!
More I'll find before I cease.
Have I told you all my flames
'Mong the amorous Syrian dames?
Have I number'd every one
Glowing under Egypt's sun?
Or the nymphs, who blushing sweet
Deck the shrine of Love in Crete;
Where the God, with festal play,
Holds eternal holiday?

Monsieur de Pauw, the author of Dissertations upon the
Greeks, is of a different opinion; he thinks, that by a capri-
cious partiality of nature, the other sex had all the beauty,
and accounts, upon this supposition, for a very singular depra-
vation of instinct among them.

Still

Still in clusters, still remain

Gade's warm, desiring train;

Still there lies a myriad more

On the sable India's shore;

These, and many far remov'd,

All are loving, all are lov'd!

Gade's warm, desiring train;] The Gaditanian girls were like the Baladiéres of India, whose dances are thus described by a French author: " Les danses sont presque toutes des pantomimes d'amour; le plan, le dessein, les attitudes, les mesures, les sons et les cadences de ces ballets, tout respire cette passion et en exprime les voluptés et les fureurs." Histoire du Commerce des Europ. dans les deux Indes. Raynal.

The music of the Gaditanian females had all the voluptuous character of their dancing, as appears from Martial:

Cantica qui Nili, qui Gaditana susurrat. Lib. iii. Epig. 63.

Lodovico Ariosto had this ode of our bard in his mind, when he wrote his poem " De diversis amoribus." See the Anthologia Italorum.

ODE

ODE XV.

TELL me, why, my sweetest dove,
Thus your humid pinions move,
Shedding through the air in showers
Essence of the balmiest flowers ?

Tell

The dove of Anacreon, bearing a letter from the poet to his
mistress, is met by a stranger, with whom this dialogue is
imagined.

The ancients made use of letter-carrying pigeons, when they
went any distance from home, as the most certain means of
conveying intelligence back. That tender domestic attach-
ment, which attracts this delicate little bird through every
danger and difficulty, till it settles in its native nest, affords to
the elegant author of " The Pleasures of Memory" a fine and
interesting exemplification of his subject.

> Led by what chart, transports the timid dove
> The wreaths of conquest, or the vows of love ?

I

See

Tell me whither, whence you rove,

Tell me all, my sweetest dove.

Curious stranger! I belong

To the bard of Teian song;

With his mandate now I fly

To the nymph of azure eye;

Ah! that eye has madden'd many,

But the poet more than any!

See the poem. Daniel Heinsius has a similar sentiment, speaking of Dousa, who adopted this method at the siege of Leyden:

Quo patriæ non tendit amor? Mandata referre

Postquam hominem nequiit mittere, misit avem.

Fuller tells us, that at the siege of Jerusalem the Christians. intercepted a letter, tied to the legs of a dove, in which the Persian Emperor promised assistance to the besieged. See Fuller's Holy War, cap. 24. book i.

Ah! that eye has madden'd many, &c.] For τυραννον, in the original, Zeune and Schneider conjecture that we should read τυραννε, in allusion to the strong influence which this object of his love held over the mind of Polycrates. See Degen.

Venus,

Venus, for a hymn of love,

Warbled in her votive grove,

('T was in sooth a gentle lay,)

Gave me to the bard away.

See me now his faithful minion,

Thus with softly-gliding pinion,

To his lovely girl I bear

Songs of passion through the air.

Oft he blandly whispers me,

" Soon, my bird, I 'll set you free."

Venus, for a hymn of love,

Warbled in her votive grove, &c.] " This passage is inva-
luable, and I do not think that any thing so beautiful or so
delicate has ever been said. What an idea does it give of the
poetry of the man, from whom Venus herself, the mother of
the Graces and the Pleasures, purchases a little hymn with one
of her favourite doves!" Longepierre.

De Pauw objects to the authenticity of this ode, because it
makes Anacreon his own panegyrist; but poets have a license
for praising themselves, which, with some indeed, may be
considered as comprised under their general privilege of fiction.

                                        But

But in vain he'll bid me fly,
I shall serve him till I die.
Never could my plumes sustain
Ruffling winds and chilling rain,
O'er the plains, or in the dell,
On the mountain's savage swell;
Seeking in the desert wood
Gloomy shelter, rustic food.
Now I lead a life of ease,
Far from such retreats as these.
From Anacreon's hand I eat
Food delicious, viands sweet;
Flutter o'er his goblet's brim,
Sip the foamy wine with him.
Then I dance and wanton round
To the lyre's beguiling sound;
Or with gently-fanning wings
Shade the minstrel while he sings:

On

On his harp then sink in slumbers,
Dreaming still of dulcet numbers!
This is all—away—away—
You have made me waste the day.
How I 've chatter'd! prating crow
Never yet did chatter so.

ODE

ODE XVI.

THOU, whose soft and rosy hues
Mimic form and soul infuse;
Best of painters! come portray
The lovely maid that's far away.

Far

This ode and the next may be called companion-pictures;
they are highly finished, and give us an excellent idea of the
taste of the ancients in beauty. Franciscus Junius quotes
them in his third book " De Pictura Veterum."

This ode has been imitated by Ronsard, Giuliano Goselini,
&c. &c. Scaliger alludes to it thus in his Anacreontica:

> Olim lepore blando,
> Litis versibus
> Candidus Anacreon
> Quam pingeret Amicus
> Descripsit Venerem suam.

Far away, my soul! thou art,

But I've thy beauties all by heart.

Paint her jetty ringlets straying,

Silky twine in tendrils playing;

And,

The Teian bard, of former days,
Attun'd his sweet descriptive lays,
And taught the painter's hand to trace
His fair beloved's every grace!

In the dialogue of Caspar Barlæus, entitled "An formosæ sit docenda," the reader will find many curious ideas and descriptions of beauty.

Thou, whose soft and rosy hues

Mimic form and soul' infuse;] I have followed the reading of the Vatican MS. ροδεας. Painting is called "the rosy art," either in reference to colouring, or as an indefinite epithet of excellence, from the association of beauty with that flower. Salvini has adopted this reading in his literal translation:

Della rosea arte signore.

The lovely maid that's far away.] If the portrait of this beauty be not merely ideal, the omission of her name is much to be regretted. Meleager, in an epigram on Anacreon, mentions "the golden Eurypyle" as his mistress.

Βιβλημενος χρυσην χειρας επ' Ευρυπυλην.

4   *Paint*

And, if painting hath the skill

To make the spicy balm distil,

Paint her jetty ringlets straying,

Silky twine in tendrils playing ;] The ancients have been very
enthusiastic in their praises of hair. Apuleius, in the second
book of his Milesiacs, says, that Venus herself, if she were
bald, though surrounded by the Graces and the Loves, could
not be pleasing even to her husband Vulcan.

Stesichorus gave the epithet καλλιπλοκαμος to the Graces,
and Simonides bestowed the same upon the Muses. See
Hadrian Junius's Dissertation upon Hair.

To this passage of our poet, Selden alluded in a note on the
Polyolbion of Drayton, song the second, where observing,
that the epithet " black-haired" was given by some of the ancients to the goddess Isis, he says, " Nor will I swear, but
that Anacreon (a man very judicious in the provoking motives
of wanton love), intending to bestow on his sweet mistress
that one of the titles of woman's special ornament, well-
haired (καλλιπλοκαμος), thought of this when he gave his
painter direction to make her black-haired."

And, if painting hath the skill

To make the spicy balm distil, &c.] Thus Philostratus, speaking of a picture: επαινω και τον ενδροσον των ροδων και φημι
γεγραφθαι αυτα μετα της οσμης. " I admire the dewiness of
these roses, and could say that their very smell was painted."

G 2   Let

Let every little lock exhale
A sigh of perfume on the gale.
Where her tresses' curly flow
Darkles o'er the brow of snow,
Let her forehead beam to light,
Burnish'd as the ivory bright.
Let her eyebrows sweetly rise
In jetty arches o'er her eyes,
Gently in a crescent gliding,
Just commingling, just dividing.
But hast thou any sparkles warm,
The lightning of her eyes to form?
Let them effuse the azure ray
With which Minerva's glances play,
And give them all that liquid fire
That Venus' languid eyes respire.
O'er her nose and cheek be shed
Flushing white and mellow'd red;

Gradual

Gradual tints, as when there glows
In snowy milk the bashful rose.

Then

And give them all that liquid fire,
That Venus' languid eyes respire.] Marchetti explains thus the
ὑγρον of the original:

> Dipingili umidetti
> Tremuli e lascivetti,
> Quai gli ha Ciprigna l'alma Dea d'Amore.

Tasso has painted in the same manner the eyes of Armida,
as La Fosse remarks:

> Qual raggio in onda le scintilla un riso
> Negli umidi occhi tremulo e lascivo.

> Within her humid, melting eyes
> A brilliant ray of laughter lies,
> Soft as the broken, solar beam,
> That trembles in the azure stream.

The mingled expression of dignity and tenderness, which
Anacreon requires the painter to infuse into the eyes of his
mistress, is more amply described in the subsequent ode.
Both descriptions are so exquisitely touched, that the artist
must have been great indeed, if he did not yield in painting
to the poet.

G 3 *Gradual*

Then her lip, so rich in blisses !

Sweet petitioner for kisses !

Pouting nest of bland persuasion,

Ripely suing Love's invasion.

Then

Gradual tints, as when there glows
In snowy milk the bashful rose.]   Thus Propertius, eleg. 3.
lib. ii.

Utque rosæ puro lacte natant folia.

And Davenant, in a little poem called " The Mistress,"
        Catch as it falls the Scythian snow,
        Bring blushing roses steep'd in milk.

Thus too Taygetus :

        Quæ lac atque rosas vincis candore rubenti.

These last words may perhaps defend the " flushing white"
of the translation.

    Then her lip, so rich in blisses !
    Sweet petitioner for kisses !]   The " lip, provoking kisses,"
in the original, is a strong and beautiful expression. Achilles
Tatius speaks of χιιλη μαλθαχα προς τα φιλημμτα, " Lips soft
and delicate for kissing."   A grave old commentator, Dionysius
Lambinus, in his notes upon Lucretius, tells us with all the
authority of experience, that girls who have large lips kiss
                                        infinitely

Then beneath the velvet chin,

Whose dimple shades a love within,

Mould her neck, with grace descending,

In a heaven of beauty ending;

While airy charms, above, below,

Sport and flutter on its snow.

infinitely sweeter than others! "Suavius viros osculantur puellæ labiosæ, quam quæ sunt brevibus labris." And Æneas Sylvius, in his tedious uninteresting story of the adulterous loves of Euryalus and Lucretia, where he particularises the beauties of the heroine (in a very false and laboured style of latinity), describes her lips as exquisitely adapted for biting. "Os parvum decensque, labia corallini coloris ad morsum aptissima." Epist. 114. lib. i.

Then beneath the velvet chin,

Whose dimple shades a love within, &c.] Madame Dacier has quoted here two pretty lines of Varro:

Sigilla in mento impressa Amoris digitulo
Vestigio demonstrant mollitudinem.

In her chin is a delicate dimple,
By the finger of Cupid imprest;
There Softness, bewitchingly simple,
Has chosen her innocent nest.

Now

Now let a floating, lucid veil,

Shadow her limbs, but not conceal;

A charm may peep, a hue may beam,

And leave the rest to Fancy's dream.

Enough—'t is she! 't is all I seek;

It glows, it lives, it soon will speak!

Now let a floating, lucid veil,
Shadow her limbs, but not conceal; &c.] This delicate art of description, which leaves imagination to complete the picture, has been seldom adopted in the imitations of this beautiful poem. Ronsard is exceptionably minute; and Politianus, in his charming portrait of a girl, full of rich and exquisite diction, has lifted the veil rather too much. The " questo che tu m' intendi" should be always left to fancy.

ODE XVII.

AND now with all thy pencil's truth,
Portray Bathyllus, lovely youth!
Let his hair, in lapses bright,
Fall like streaming rays of light;
And there the raven's die confuse
With the yellow sunbeam's hues.

The reader, who wishes to acquire an accurate idea of the
judgment of the ancients in beauty, will be indulged by consulting Junius de Pictura Veterum, ninth chapter, third book,
where he will find a very curious selection of descriptions and
epithets of personal perfections; he compares this ode with a
description of Theodoric, king of the Goths, in the second
epistle, first book of Sidonius Appollinaris.

Let his hair, in lapses bright,

Fall like streaming rays of light; &c.] He here describes
the sunny hair; "the flava coma," which the ancients so much
admired. The Romans gave this colour artificially to their
hair. See Stanisl. Kobienzyck de Luxu Romanorum.

Let

Let not the braid, with artful twine,
The flowing of his locks confine;
But loosen every golden ring,
To float upon the breeze's wing.
Beneath the front of polish'd glow,
Front, as fair as mountain-snow,
And guileless as the dews of dawn,
Let the majestic brows be drawn,

Let not the braid, with artful twine, &c.] If the original here, which is particularly beautiful, can admit of any additional value, that value is conferred by Gray's admiration of it. See his letters to West.

Some annotators have quoted on this passage the description of Photis's hair in Apuleius; but nothing can be more distant from the simplicity of our poet's manner, than that affectation of richness which distinguishes the style of Apuleius.

Front, as fair as mountain-snow,

And guileless as the dews of dawn, &c.] Torrentius, upon the words " insignem tenui fronte," in the thirty-third ode of the first book of Horace, is of opinion that " tenui" bears the meaning of απαλον here; but he is certainly incorrect.

Of

Of ebon dies, enrich'd by gold,

Such as the scaly snakes unfold.

Mingle, in his jetty glances,

Power that awes, and love that trances;

Steal

Mingle, in his jetty glances,

Power that awes, and love that trances; &c.] Tasso gives a similar character to the eyes of Clorinda:

> Lampeggiar gli occhi, e folgorar gli sguardi
> Dolci ne l'ira.

> Her eyes were glowing with a heavenly heat,
> Emaning fire, and e'en in anger sweet!

The poetess Veronica Cambara is more diffuse upon this variety of expression:

> Occhi lucenti e belli
> Come esser puo ch' in un medesmo istante
> Nascan de voi si nove forme et tante?
> Lieti, mesti, superbi, humil' altieri
> Vi mostrate in un punto, ondi di speme,
> Et di timor de empiete, &c. &c.

> Oh! tell me, brightly-beaming eye,
> Whence in your little orbit lie
> So many different traits of fire,
> Expressing each a new desire.

Now

Steal from Venus bland desire,

Steal from Mars the look of fire,

Blend them in such expression here,

That we by turns may hope and fear!

Now from the sunny apple seek

The velvet down that spreads his cheek;

And there let Beauty's rosy ray

In flying blushes richly play;

Blushes, of that celestial flame

Which lights the cheek of virgin shame.

Then for his lips, that ripely gem—

But let thy mind imagine them!

> Now with angry scorn you darkle,
> 'Now with tender languish sparkle,
> And we who view the various mirror,
> Feel at once both hope and terror.

Monsieur Chevreau, citing the lines of our poet, in his critique on the poems of Malherbe, produces a Latin version of them from a manuscript which he had seen, entitled " Joan. Falconis Anacreontici Lusus."

Paint,

Paint, where the ruby cell uncloses,

Persuasion sleeping upon roses ;

And give his lip that speaking air,

As if a word was hovering there !

His neck of ivory splendour trace,

Moulded with soft but manly grace;

Fair as the neck of Paphia's boy,

Where Paphia's arms have hung in joy.

Persuasion sleeping upon roses ;]　It was worthy of the delicate imagination of the Greeks to deify Persuasion, and give her the lips for her throne.　We are here reminded of a very interesting fragment of Anacreon, preserved by the scholiast upon Pindar, and supposed to belong to a poem reflecting with some severity on Simonides, who was the first, we are told, that ever made a hireling of his muse.

Ουδ' αργυρεη κοτ' ελαμψε Πειθω.

Nor yet had fair Persuasion shone
In silver splendours, not her own.

And give his lip that speaking air,
As if a word was hovering there !]　In the original λαλων σιωπη.　The mistress of Petrarch " parla con silentio," which is perhaps the best method of female eloquence.

Give

Give him the winged Hermes' hand,
With which he waves his snaky wand;
Let Bacchus then the breast supply,
And Leda's son the sinewy thigh.
But oh! suffuse his limbs of fire
With all that glow of young desire,

Which

Give him the winged Hermes' hand, &c.] In Shakespeare's
Cymbeline there is a similar method of description:

———this is his hand,
His foot mercurial, his martial thigh,
The brawns of Hercules.

We find it likewise in Hamlet. Longepierre thinks that the
hands of Mercury are selected by Anacreon, on account of the
graceful gestures which were supposed to characterize the god
of eloquence; but Mercury was also the patron of thieves, and
may perhaps be praised as a light-fingered deity.

But oh! suffuse his limbs of fire
With all that glow of young desire, &c.] I have taken the
liberty here of somewhat veiling the original. Madame Dacier,
in her translation, has hung out lights (as Sterne would call it)
at this passage. It is very much to be regretted, that this sub-
stitution of asterisks has been so much adopted in the popular
interpretations

Which kindles, when the wishful sigh
Steals from the heart, unconscious why.
Thy pencil, though divinely bright,
Is envious of the eye's delight,
Or its enamour'd touch would shew
His shoulder, fair as sunless snow,
Which now in veiling shadow lies,
Remov'd from all but Fancy's eyes.
Now, for his feet—but hold—forbear—
I see a godlike portrait there;

So

interpretations of the Classics; it serves but to bring whatever
is exceptionable into notice, " claramque facem præferre
pudendis."

————But hold—forbear—
I see a godlike portrait there; &c.] This is very spirited, but
it requires explanation. While the artist is pursuing the portrait of Bathyllus, Anacreon, we must suppose, turns round
and sees a picture of Apollo, which was intended for an altar
at Samos; he instantly tells the painter to cease his work;
that this picture will serve for Bathyllus; and that, when he

goes

171265

So like Bathyllus!—sure there's none
So like Bathyllus but the Sun!
Oh! let this pictur'd god be mine,
And keep the boy for Samos' shrine;
Phœbus shall then Bathyllus be,
Bathyllus then the deity!

goes to Samos, he may make an Apollo of the portrait of the
boy which he had begun.

"Bathyllus (says Madame Dacier) could not be more ele-
gantly praised, and this one passage does him more honour
than the statue, however beautiful it might be, which Polycrates raised to him."

ODE

ODE XVIII.

Now the star of day is high,
Fly, my girls, in pity fly, —
Bring me wine in brimming urns,
Cool my lip, it burns, it burns!
Sunn'd by the meridian fire,
Panting, languid I expire!

"An elegant translation of this ode may be found in Ramler's Lyr. Blumenlese, lib. v. p. 403." Degen.

Bring me wine in brimming urns, &c.] Orig. οινον αμυστι.
"The amystis was a method of drinking used among the
Thracians. Thus Horace, 'Threicià vincat amystide." Mad.
Dacier, Longepierre, &c. &c.

Parrhasius, in his twenty-sixth epistle (Thesaur. Critic.
vol. i.), explains the amystis as a draught to be exhausted
without drawing breath, " uno haustu." A note in the margin of this epistle of Parrhasius says, " Politianus vestem esse
putabat," but I cannot find where.

Give me all those humid flowers,

Drop them o'er my brow in showers.

Scarce a breathing chaplet now

Lives upon my feverish brow;

Give me all those humid flowers, &c.] By the original reading of this line, the poet says, " Give me the flower of wine"— Date flosculos Lyæi, as it is in the version of Elias Andreas ; and

Deh porgetimi del fiore

Di quel almo e buon liquore,

as Regnier has it, who supports the reading. Αγθος would undoubtedly bear this application, which is somewhat similar to its import in the epigram of Simonides upon Sophocles :

Εσβεσθη γιραμ Σοφοκλεις, ανθος αοιδην.

And flos in the Latin is frequently applied in this manner— thus Cethegus is called by Ennius, Flos illibatus populi, suadæque medulla, " The immaculate flower of the people, and the very marrow of persuasion," in those verses cited by Aulus Gellius, lib. xii. which Cicero praised, and Seneca thought ridiculous.

But in the passage before us, if we admit ικμηαν, according to Faber's conjecture, the sense is sufficiently clear, and we need not have recourse to refinements.

Every

Every dewy rose I wear

Sheds its tears, and withers there.

Every dewy rose I wear
Sheds its tears, and withers there.] There are some beautiful
lines, by Angerianus, upon a garland, which I cannot resist
quoting here:

Ante fores madidæ sic sic pendete corollæ,
    Mane orto imponet Cælia vos capiti;
At quum per niveam cervicem influxerit humor,
    Dicite, non roris sed pluvia hæc lacrimæ.

By Celia's arbour all the night
Hang, humid wreath, the lover's vow;
And haply, at the morning light,
My love shall twine thee round her brow.

Then, if upon her bosom bright
Some drops of dew shall fall from thee,
Tell her, they are not drops of night,
But tears of sorrow shed by me!

In the poem of Mr. Sheridan's, "Uncouth is this moss-
covered grotto of stone," there is an idea very singularly coin-
cident with this of Angerianus, in the stanza which begins,

And thou, stony grot, in thy arch mayst preserve.

But for you, my burning mind!

Oh! what shelter shall I find?

Can the bowl, or flowret's dew,

Cool the flame that scorches you?

But for you, my burning mind! &c.] The transition here is peculiarly delicate and impassioned; but the commentators have perplexed the sentiment by a variety of readings and conjectures.

ODE

ODE XIX.

Here recline you, gentle maid;
Sweet is this imbowering shade;
Sweet the young, the modest trees,
Ruffled by the kissing breeze;

Sweet

The description of this bower is so natural and animated,
that we cannot help feeling a degree of coolness and freshness
while we read it. Longepierre has quoted from the first book
of the Anthologia the following epigram, as somewhat re-
sembling this ode:

Ερχεο και κατ' εμαν ιζευ πιτυν, α τε μελιχρον
Προς μαλακες ηχει κεκλιμενα ζεφυρες.
Ηνιδε και χρονισμα μελιςωγες, ενθα μελισδων
Ηδον ερημαιαις ύπνον αγω καλαμοις.

Come, sit by the shadowy pine
That covers my sylvan retreat;
And see how the branches incline
The breathing of zephyr to meet.

H 3. See

Sweet the little founts that weep,

Lulling bland the mind to sleep ;

Hark ! they whisper as they roll,

Calm persuasion to the soul ;

Tell

See the fountain, that, flowing, diffuses

Around me a glittering spray ;

By its brink, as the traveller muses,

I sooth him to sleep with my lay !

Here recline you, gentle maid, &c.] The Vatican MS. reads βαθυλλε, which renders the whole poem metaphorical. Some commentator suggests the reading of βαθυλλον, which makes a pun upon the name ; a grace that Plato himself has condescended to in writing of his boy αγρ. See the epigram of this philosopher, which I quote on the twenty-second ode.

There is another epigram by this philosopher, preserved in Laertius, which turns upon the same word.

Αστηρ πριν μεν ελαμπες ενι ζωοισιν εωος

Νυν δε θανων, λαμπεις εσπερος εν φθιμενοις.

In life thou wert my morning-star,

But now that death has stol'n thy light,

Alas ! thou shinest dim and far,

Like the pale beam that weeps at night.

In

Tell me, tell me, is not this
All a stilly scene of bliss?
Who, my girl, would pass it by?
Surely neither you nor I!

In the Veneres Blyenburgicæ, under the head of " allu-
siones," we find a number of such frigid conceits upon names,
selected from the poets of the middle ages.

Who, my girl, would pass it by?

Surely neither you nor I!] What a finish he gives to the picture by the simple exclamation of the original! In these delicate turns he is inimitable; and yet, hear what a French
translator says on the passage: " This conclusion appeared to
me too trifling after such a description, and I thought proper
to add somewhat to the strength of the original."

ODE

ODE XX.

ONE day, the Muses twin'd the hands
Of baby Love, with flow'ry bands;
And to celestial Beauty gave
The captive infant as her slave.

His

By this allegory of the Muses making Cupid the prisoner of
Beauty, Anacreon seems to insinuate the softening influence
which a cultivation of poetry has over the mind, in making it
peculiarly susceptible to the impressions of beauty.

Though in the following epigram, by the philosopher Plato,
which is found in the third book of Diogenes Laertius, the
Muses are made to disavow all the influence of Love.

'Α Κυπρις Μυσαισι, κορασια ταν Αφροδιταν
Τιματ' η τον Ερωτα υμμιν εφοπλισομαι.
'Αι Μοισαι ποτι Κυπριν. Αρει τα φωμυλα ταυτα
'Ημιν ν πιπται τυτο το παιδαριον.

" Yield to my gentle power, Parnassian maids;"
Thus to the Muses spoke the Queen of Charms—
" Or Love shall flutter in your classic shades,
" And make your grove the camp of Paphian arms!"

" No,"

His mother comes with many a toy,
To ransom her beloved boy;

His

"No," said the virgins of the tuneful bower,
"We scorn thine own and all thy urchin's art;
"Though Mars has trembled at the infant's power,
"His shaft is pointless o'er a Muse's heart!"

There is a sonnet by Benedetto Guidi, the thought of which was suggested by this ode.

Scherzava dentro all' auree chiome Amore
Dell' alma donna della vita mia:
E tanta era il piacer ch' ei ne sentia,
Che non sapea, né volea uscirne fore.

Quando ecco ivi annodar si sente il core,
Si, che per forza ancor convien che stia:
Tai lacci alta beltate orditi avia
Del crespo crin, per farsi eterno onore.

Onde offre infin dal ciel degna mercede,
A chi scioglie il figliuol la bella dea
Da tanti nodi, in ch' ella stretto il vede.
Ma ei vinto a due occhi l' arme cede:
Et t' affatichi indarno, Citerea;
Che s' altri 'l scioglie, egli a legar si riede..

Love,

His mother sees, but all in vain!

He ne'er will leave his chains again.

Nay,

Love, wandering through the golden maze
  Of my beloved's hair,
Trac'd every lock with fond delays,
  And, doting, linger'd there.

And soon he found 't were vain to fly,
  His heart was close confin'd;
And every curlet was a tie,
  A chain by Beauty twin'd.

Now Venus seeks her boy's release,
  With ransom from above:
But, Venus! let thy efforts cease,
  For Love's the slave of love.
And, should we loose his golden chain,
The prisoner would return again!

His mother comes, with many a toy,
To ransom her beloved boy; &c.] Venus thus proclaims the reward for her fugitive child in the first idyll of Moschus:

'Ο μανυτας γερας ἑξει,

Μισθος τοι, τα φιλαμα το Κυπριδος. ην δ' αγαγης νιν

Ου γυμνον το φιλαμα, τυ δ' ω ξενε, και πλεον ἑξεις.

5

On

Nay, should they take his chains away,
The little captive still would stay.
" If this," he cries, " a bondage be,
" Who could wish for liberty ?"

On him, who the haunts of my Cupid can show,
A kiss of the tenderest stamp I 'll bestow ;
But he, who can bring me the wanderer here,
Shall have something more rapturous, something more dear.

This " something more" is the quidquid post oscula dulce of
Secundus.

After this ode, there follow in the Vatican MS. these extra-
ordinary lines :

Ηδυμιλης Αναχριων
Ηδυμιλης δι Σατφω
Πινδαρικον το δι μοι μιλος
Συγκιρασας τις ιγχιοι
Τα τρια ταυτα μοι δοκιι
Και Διονυσος ιισιλθων
Και Παφιη παραχροος
Και αυτος Ερως καν ιωιιιν

These lines, which appear to me to have as little sense as
metre, are most probably the interpolation of the transcriber.

ODE

ODE XXI.

OBSERVE when mother earth is dry,
She drinks the droppings of the sky;
And then the dewy cordial gives
To ev'ry thirsty plant that lives.

The

The commentators who have endeavoured to throw the chains of precision over the spirit of this beautiful trifle, require too much from Anacreontic philosophy. Monsieur Gail very wisely thinks that the poet uses the epithet μελαιναν, because black earth absorbs moisture more quickly than any other; and accordingly he indulges us with an experimental disquisition on the subject. See Gail's notes.

One of the Capilupi has imitated this ode, in an epitaph on a drunkard:

Dum vixi sine fine bibi, sic imbrifer arcus
  Sic tellus pluvias sole perusta bibit.
Sic bibit assiduè fontes et flumina Pontus,
  Sic semper sitiens Sol maris haurit aquas.

Re,

The vapours, which at evening weep,
Are beverage to the swelling deep;

And

Ne te igitur jactes plus me, Silene, bibisse;
Et mihi da victas tu quoque, Bacche, manus.

Hippolytus Capilupus.

While life was mine, the little hour
In drinking still unvaried flew;
I drank as earth imbibes the shower,
Or as the rainbow drinks the dew;
As ocean quaffs the rivers up,
Or flushing sun inhales the sea:
Silenus trembled at my cup,
And Bacchus was outdone by me!

I cannot omit citing those remarkable lines of Shakespeare, where the thoughts of the ode before us are preserved with such striking similitude:

TIMON, ACT IV.

I 'll example you with thievery.
The sun 's a thief, and with his great attraction
Robs the vast sea. The moon 's an arrant thief,
And her pale fire she snatches from the sun.
The sea 's a thief, whose liquid surge resolves

The

And when the rosy sun appears,
He drinks the ocean's misty tears.
The moon too quaffs her paly stream
Of lustre, from the solar beam.
Then, hence with all your sober thinking!
Since Nature's holy law is drinking;
I 'll make the laws of nature mine,
And pledge the universe in wine!

The mounds into salt tears. The earth's a thief,
That feeds, and breeds by a composture stol'n
From general excrements.

ODE

ODE XXII.

THE Phrygian rock, that braves the storm,
Was once a weeping matron's form;
And Progne, hapless, frantic maid,
Is now a swallow in the shade.

                                  Oh!

Ogilvie, in his Essay on the Lyric Poetry of the Ancients, in remarking upon the Odes of Anacreon, says, " In some of his pieces there is exuberance and even wildness of imagination; in that particularly, which is addressed to a young girl, where he wishes alternately to be transformed to a mirror, a coat, a stream, a bracelet, and a pair of shoes, for the different purposes which he recites: this is mere sport and wontonness."

It is the wantonness however of a very graceful Muse; ludit amabiliter. The compliment of this ode is exquisitely delicate, and so singular for the period in which Anacreon lived, when the scale of love had not yet been graduated into all its little progressive refinements, that if we were inclined to question the authenticity of the poem, we should find a much more plausible argument in the features of modern gallantry which

Oh! that a mirror's form were mine,
To sparkle with that smile divine;
And like my heart I then should be,
Reflecting thee, and only thee!

Or

which it bears, than in any of those fastidious conjectures upon
which some commentators have presumed so far. Degen
thinks it spurious, and De Pauw pronounces it to be miserable.
Longepierre and Barnes refer us to several imitations of this
ode, from which I shall only select an epigram of Dionysius.

Ειθ' ανιμος γινομην, συ δε γι στιχουσα παρ' αυγαι,
    Στηθια γυμνωσαις, και με πνιοντα λαβοις.
Ειθι ροδον γινομην υποπορφυρον, οφρα με χερσιν
    Αραμενη, κομισαις στηθισι χιονιοις.
Ειθι κρινον γινομην λιυκοχροον, οφρα με χερσιν
    Αραμενη, μαλλον σης χροτης κορισης.

I wish I could like zephyr steal
    To wanton o'er thy mazy vest;
And thou wouldst ope thy bosom-veil,
    And take me panting to thy breast!

I wish I might a rose-bud grow,
    And thou wouldst cull me from the bower,
And place me on that breast of snow,
    Where I should bloom, a wintry flower.

I wish

Or were I, love, the robe which flows
O'er every charm that secret glows,
In many a lucid fold to swim,
And cling and grow to every limb!

I wish I were the lily's leaf,
　To fade upon that bosom warm ;
There I should wither, pale and brief,
　The trophy of thy fairer form !

Allow me to add, that Plato has expressed as fanciful a wish
in a distich preserved by Laertius :

Αςερας εισαθρεις, αςηρ εμος. ειθε γενοιμην
Ουρανος, ως πολλοις ομμασιν εις σε βλεπω.

TO STELLA.

Why dost thou gaze upon the sky ?
　Oh ! that I were that spangled sphere,
And every star should be an eye,
　To wonder on thy beauties here !

Apuleius quotes this epigram of the divine philosopher, to
justify himself for his verses on Critias and Charipus.　See his
Apology, where he also adduces the example of Anacreon ;
" Fecere tamen et alii talia, et si vos ignoratis, apud Græcos
Teius quidam, &c. &c."

Oh ! could I, as the streamlet's wave,
Thy warmly-mellowing beauties lave,
Or float as perfume on thine hair,
And breathe my soul in fragrance there !
I wish I were the zone, that lies
Warm to thy breast, and feels its sighs !
Or like those envious pearls that show
So faintly round that neck of snow,

I wish I were the zone, that lies
Warm to thy breast, and feels its sighs] This ταινιν was a
riband, or band, called by the Romans fascia and strophium,
which the women wore for the purpose of restraining the exuberance of the bosom. Vide Polluc. Onomast. Thus Martial :

    Fasciâ crescentes dominæ compesce papillas.

The women of Greece not only wore this zone, but con-
demned themselves to fasting, and made use of certain drugs
and powders, for the same purpose. To these expedients they
were compelled, in consequence of their inelegant fashion of
compressing the waist into a very narrow compass, which ne-
cessarily caused an excessive tumidity in the bosom. See
Dioscorides, lib. v.

Yes, I would be a happy gem,

Like them to hang, to fade like them.

What more would thy Anacreon be?

Oh! any thing that touches thee.

Nay, sandals for those airy feet—

Thus to be press'd by thee were sweet!

Nay, sandals for those airy feet—

Thus to be press'd by thee were sweet!] The sophist Philostratus, in one of his love-letters, has borrowed this thought; ω αδετοι ποδις. ω καλλος ελευθερος. ω τρισευδαιμων εγω και μακαριος εαν πατησιτε με. "Oh lovely feet! oh excellent beauty! oh! thrice happy and blessed should I be, if you would but tread on me!" In Shakespeare, Romeo desires to be a glove:

Oh! that I were a glove upon that hand,

That I might kiss that cheek!

And, in his Passionate Pilgrim, we meet with an idea somewhat like that of the thirteenth line:

He, spying her, bounc'd in, where as he stood,

"O Jove!" quoth she, "why was not I a flood?"

In Burton's Anatomy of Melancholy, that whimsical farrago of "all such reading as was never read," there is a very old translation of this ode, before 1632. "Englished by Mr. B. Holiday in his Technog. act 1. scene 7."

ODE XXIII.

I OFTEN wish this languid lyre,
This warbler of my soul's desire,
Could raise the breath of song sublime,
To men of fame, in former time.

This ode is first in the series of all the editions, and is
thought to be peculiarly designed as an introduction to the
rest; it however characterizes the genius of the Teian but very
inadequately, as wine, the burden of his lays, is not even
mentioned in it.

　　　——cum multo Venerem confundere mero
　　Precepit Lyrici Teia Musa senis.　　　Ovid.

The twenty-sixth Ode συ μεν λεγεις τα Θηβης, might, with
as much propriety, be the harbinger of his songs.

Bion has expressed the sentiments of the ode before us with
much simplicity in his fourth idyll. I have given it rather pa-
raphrastically; it has been so frequently translated, that I
could not otherwise avoid triteness and repetition.

But

But when the soaring theme I try,
Along the chords my numbers die,
And whisper, with dissolving tone,
" Our sighs are given to love alone!"
Indignant at the feeble lay,
I tore the panting chords away,
Attun'd them to a nobler swell,
And struck again the breathing shell;
In all the glow of epic fire,
To Hercules I wake the lyre!
But still its fainting sighs repeat,
" The tale of love alone is sweet!"

Then

In all the glow of epic fire,

To Hercules I wake the lyre!] Madame Dacier generally
translates λυρη into a lute, which I believe is rather inaccurate.
" D'expliquer la lyre des anciens (says Monsieur Sorel) par un
luth, c'est ignorer la différence qu'il y a entre ces deux instru-
mens de musique." Bibliotheque Françoise.

But still its fainting sighs repeat,

" *The tale of love alone is sweet!*"] The word ετιφωνιι, in

the

Then fare thee well, seductive dream,

That mad'st me follow Glory's theme;

For thou my lyre, and thou my heart,

Shall never more in spirit part;

And thou the flame shalt feel as well

As thou the flame shalt sweetly tell!

the original, may imply that kind of musical dialogue prac-
tised by the ancients, in which the lyre was made to respond
to the questions proposed by the singer. This was a method
which Sappho used, as we are told by Hermogenes: " ὅταν
την λυραν ερωτα Σαπφω και ὁταν αυτη αποκρινεται." Περι Ιδεω.
Τομ. δευτ.

ODE XXIV.

To all that breathe the airs of heaven,
Some boon of strength has Nature given.
When the majestic bull was born,
She fenc'd his brow with wreathed horn.

She

Henry Stephen has imitated the idea of this ode in the following lines of one of his poems:

Provida dat cunctis Natura animantibus arma,
    Et sua fæmineum possidet arma genus,
Ungulâque ut defendit equum, atque ut cornua taurum,
    Armata est formâ fæmina pulchra suâ.

And the same thought occurs in those lines, spoken by Corisca in Pastor Fido:

Cosi noi la bellezza
Ch 'é vertu nostra cosi propria, come
La forza del leone
E l'ingegno de l'huomo.

The

She arm'd the courser's foot of air,

And wing'd with speed the panting hare.

She gave the lion fangs of terror,

And, on the ocean's crystal mirror,

Taught the unnumber'd scaly throng

To trace their liquid path along;

While for the umbrage of the grove,

She plum'd the warbling world of love,

To man she gave the flame refin'd,

The spark of heav'n—a thinking mind!

And

> The lion boasts his savage powers,
> And lordly man his strength of mind;
> But beauty's charm is solely ours,
> Peculiar boon, by Heav'n assign'd!

" An elegant explication of the beauties of this ode (says Degen) may be found in Grimm en den Anmerkk. Veber einige Oden des Anakr."

To man she gave the flame refin'd,

The spark of heav'n—a thinking mind. In my first attempt to translate this ode, I had interpreted φρονημα, with Baxter

and

And had she no surpassing treasure,
For thee, oh woman! child of pleasure?
She gave thee beauty—shaft of eyes,
That every shaft of war outflies!
She gave thee beauty—blush of fire,
That bids the flames of war retire!

Woman!

and Barnes, as implying courage and military virtue; but I do
not think that the gallantry of the idea suffers by the import
which I have now given to it. For, why need we consider
this possession of wisdom as exclusive? and in truth, as the
design of Anacreon is to estimate the treasure of beauty, above
all the rest which Nature has distributed, it is perhaps even
refining upon the delicacy of the compliment, to prefer the
radiance of female charms to the cold illumination of wisdom
and prudence; and to think that women's eyes are

————the books, the academies,
From whence doth spring the true Promethean fire.

She gave thee beauty—shaft of eyes,
That every shaft of war outflies!] Thus Achilles Tatius:
καλλος οξυτερον τιτρωσκει βελος και δια των οφθαλμων εις την
ψυχην καταρρει. Οφθαλμος γαρ ἑδος ερωτικη τραυματι. "Beauty
wounds

Woman ! be fair, we must adore thee ;
Smile, and a world is weak before thee !

wounds more swiftly than the arrow, and passes through the
eye to the very soul ; for the eye is the inlet to the wounds of
love."

Woman! be fair, we must adore thee ;

Smile, and a world is weak before thee !] Longepierre's remark here is very ingenious: " The Romans," says he,
" were so convinced of the power of beauty, that they used
a word implying strength in the place of the epithet beautiful.
Thus Plautus, act 2. scene 2. Bacchid.

Sed Bacchis etiam fortis tibi visa.

' Fortis, id est formosa,' say Servius and Nonius."

ODE XXV.

Once in each revolving year,
Gentle bird! we find thee here.
When Nature wears her summer-vest,
Thou com'st to weave thy simple nest;
But when the chilling winter lowers,
Again thou seek'st the genial bowers
Of Memphis, or the shores of Nile,
Where sunny hours of verdure smile.

This is another ode addressed to the swallow. Alberti has
imitated both in one poem, beginning

Perch' io pianga al tuo canto
Rondinella importuna, &c.

And

And thus thy wing of freedom roves,
Alas ! unlike the plumed loves,
That linger in this hapless breast,
And never, never change their nest !

Still

Alas! unlike the plumed loves,
That linger in this hapless breast,
And never, never change their nest.] Thus Love is repre-
sented as a bird, in an epigram cited by Longepierre from the
Anthologia :

Αιει μοι δυνει μεν εν ωασιν ηχος ερωτος,
  Ομμα δε σιγα ποθοις το γλυκυ δακρυ φερει.
Ουδ' η νυξ, ου φεγγος εκοιμισεν, αλλ' υπο φιλτρων
  Ηδη που κραδιη γνωρος ενεςι τυπος.
Ω πτανοι, μη και ποτ' εφιπτασθαι μεν ερωτες
  Οιδατ', αποπτηναι δ' ουδ' οσον ισχυετε ;

'T is Love that murmurs in my breast,
  And makes me shed the secret tear ;
Nor day nor night my heart has rest,
  For night and day his voice I hear.

A wound within my heart I find,
  And oh ! 't is plain where Love has been ;
For still he leaves a wound behind,
  Such as within my heart is seen.

Oh

Still every year, and all the year,
A flight of loves engender here;
And some their infant plumage try,
And on a tender winglet fly;
While in the shell, impregn'd with fires,
Cluster a thousand more desires;
Some from their tiny prisons peeping,
And some in formless embryo sleeping.
My bosom, like the vernal groves,
Resounds with little warbling loves;
One urchin imps the other's feather,
Then twin-desires they wing together,
And still as they have learn'd to soar,
The wanton babies teem with more.

    Oh bird of Love! with song so drear,
      Make not my soul the nest of pain;
    Oh! let the wing which brought thee here,
      In pity waft thee hence again!

                              But

But is there then no kindly art,
To chase these cupids from my heart?
No, no! I fear, alas! I fear
They will for ever nestle here!

ODE

ODE XXVI.

THY harp may sing of Troy's alarms,
Or tell the tale of Theban arms;
With other wars my song shall burn,
For other wounds my harp shall mourn.
'T was not the crested warrior's dart,
Which drank the current of my heart;
Nor naval arms, nor mailed steed,
Have made this vanquish'd bosom bleed;
No—from an eye of liquid blue,
A host of quiver'd cupids flew;

And

"The German poet Uz has imitated this ode. Compare also Weisse Scherz. Lieder. lib. iii. der Soldat." Gail, Degen.

No—from an eye of liquid blue,
A host of quiver'd cupids flew;] Longepierre has quoted part
of

And now my heart all bleeding lies
Beneath this army of the eyes !

of an epigram from the seventh book of the Anthologia, which
has a fancy something like this :

———Ου μη λελαθας

Τοξοτα, Ζηιοφιλης ομμαπ κρυπτομενος.

Archer Love ! though slily creeping,
    Well I know where thou dost lie ;
I saw thee through the curtain peeping,
    That fringes Zenophelia's eye.

The poets abound with conceits on the archery of the eyes,
but few have turned the thought so naturally as Anacreon.
Ronsard gives to the eyes of his mistress " un petit camp
d'amours."

ODE

ODE XXVII.

WE read the flying courser's name
Upon his side in marks of flame;
And, by their turban'd brows alone,
The warriors of the East are known.
But in the lover's glowing eyes,
The inlet to his bosom lies;

Through

This ode forms a part of the preceding in the Vatican MS.
but I have conformed to the editions in translating them sepa-
rately.

" Compare with this (says Degen) the poem of Ramler
Wahrzeichen der Liebe, in Lyr. Blumenlese, lib. iv. p. 313."

But in the lover's glowing eyes,

The inlet to his bosom lies;] " We cannot see into the heart,"
says Madame Dacier. But the lover answers—

Il cor ne gli occhi et ne la fronte ho scritto.

Through them we see the small faint mark,
Where Love has dropp'd his burning spark !

Monsieur La Fosse has given the following lines, as enlarg-
ing on the thought of Anacreon :

> Lorsque je vois un amant,
> Il cache en vain son tourment,
> A le trahir tout conspire,
> Sa langueur, son embarras,
> Tout ce qu'il peut faire ou dire,
> Même ce qu'il ne dit pas.

In vain the lover tries to veil
  The flame which in his bosom lies ;
His cheeks' confusion tells the tale,
  We read it in his languid eyes :
And though his words the heart betray,
His silence speaks e'en more than they.

ODE

ODE XXVIII.

As in the Lemnian caves of fire,
The mate of her who nurs'd desire
Moulded the glowing steel, to form
Arrows for Cupid, thrilling warm;
While Venus every barb imbues
With droppings of her honied dews;
And Love (alas the victim-heart!)
Tinges with gall the burning dart;

Once,

·This ode is referred to by La Mothe le Vayer, who, I believe, was the author of that curious little work, called
" Hexameron Rustique." He makes use of this, as well as
the thirty-fifth, in his ingenious but indelicate explanation of
Homer's Cave of the Nymphs. Journée Quatrieme.

While Love (alas the victim-heart!)
Tinges with gall the burning dart;] Thus Claudian—

K 2   Labuntur

Once, to this Lemnian cave of flame,
The crested Lord of battles came;
'T was from the ranks of war he rush'd,
His spear with many a life-drop blush'd!

He

Labuntur gemini fontes, hic dulcis, amarus
Alter, et infusis corrumpit mella venenis,
Unde Cupidineas armavit fama sagittas.

In Cyprus' isle two rippling fountains fall,
And one with honey flows, and one with gall:
In these, if we may take the tale from fame,
The son of Venus dips his darts of flame.

See the ninety-first emblem of Alciatus, on the close connexion which subsists between sweets and bitterness. Apes ideo pungunt (says Petronius) quia ubi dulce, ibi et acidum invenies.

The allegorical description of Cupid's employment, in Horace, may vie with this before us in fancy, though not in delicacy:

———ferus et Cupido
Semper ardentes acuens sagittas
Cote cruentâ.

And Cupid, sharpening all his fiery darts,
Upon a whetstone stain'd with blood of hearts.

Secundus

He saw the mystic darts, and smil'd
Derision on the archer-child.
" And dost thou smile ?" said little Love ;
" Take this dart, and thou mayst prove,
" That though they pass the breeze's flight,
" My bolts are not so feathery light."
He took the shaft—and oh ! thy look,
Sweet Venus ! when the shaft he took—
He sigh'd, and felt the urchin's art ;
He sigh'd, in agony of heart,
" It is not light—I die with pain !
" Take—take thy arrow back again."
" No," said the child, " it must not be,
" That little dart was made for thee !"

Secundus has borrowed this, but has somewhat softened the
image by the omission of the epithet " cruentâ :"

Fallor an ardentes acuebat cote sagittas ?   Eleg. 1.

K 3   ODE

ODE XXIX.

Yes—loving is a painful thrill,
And not to love more painful still;
But surely 't is the worst of pain,
To love and not be lov'd again !

Affection

Yes—loving is a painful thrill,
And not to love more painful still; &c.] Monsieur Menage,
in the following Anacreontic, enforces the necessity of loving.

Περι τυ δειν φιλησαι.

  Προς Πετρον Δανιηλα 'Υττον.

Μεγα θαυμα των αοιδων

Χαριτων θαλος 'Υττι,

Φιλιωμεν ω έταιρι.

Φιλησαν δι σοφιςαι.

Φιλησι σεμνος ανηρ,

Το τικτον τυ Σωφρονισκυ,

Σωφιης ωατηρ απασης.

T.

Affection now has fled from earth,
Nor fire of genius, light of birth,
Nor heavenly virtue, can beguile
From beauty's cheek one favouring smile.

Gold

Τι δ' ανευ γενοιτ' Ερωτος ;
Αχοτη μεν εςι ψυχης *.
Πτερυγεσσιν εις Ολυμπον
Καταχειμενυς αναιρει.
Βραδιας τετηγμανοισι
Βελεσσιν εξαγειρει.
Πυρι λαμπαδος φαεινω
Ρυπαρωτερυς καθαιρει.
Φιλευμεν υν ᾽ΥΕΤΤΕ₂
Φιλευμεν ω ἑταιρε.
Αδιχως δε λοιδορωντι
Αγιυς ερωτας ημων
Κακον ευξομαι το μισον
Ἱνα μη δυναιτ' εχεινος
Φιλειν τι και φιλεισθαι.

* This line is borrowed from an epigram by Alpheus of Mitylene :

———ψυχης εςιν Ερως αχοτη.

Menage, I think, says somewhere, that he was the first who produced this epigram to the world.

K 4

TO

Gold is the woman's only theme,

Gold is the woman's only dream.

Oh! never be that wretch forgiven—

Forgive him not, indignant heaven!

Whose

TO PETER DANIEL HUETT.

Thou! of tuneful bards the first,
Thou! by all the graces nurst;
Friend! each other friend above,
Come with me, and learn to love.
Loving is a simple lore,
Graver men have learn'd before;
Nay, the boast of former ages,
Wisest of the wisest sages,
Sophroniscus' prudent son,
Was by love's illusion won.
Oh! how heavy life would move,
If we knew not how to love!
Love's a whetstone to the mind;
Thus 't is pointed, thus refin'd.
When the soul dejected lies,
Love can waft it to the skies;

When

Whose grovelling eyes could first adore,

Whose heart could pant for sordid ore,

Since that devoted thirst began,

Man has forgot to feel for man ;

The pulse of social life is dead,

And all its fonder feelings fled !

When in languor sleeps the heart,
Love can wake it with his dart ;
When the mind is dull and dark,
Love can light it with his spark.
Come, oh ! come then, let us haste
All the bliss of love to taste ;
Let us love both night and day,
Let us love our lives away !
And when hearts, from loving free,
(If indeed such hearts there be,)
Frown upon our gentle flame,
And the sweet delusion blame ;
This shall be my only curse,
(Could I, could I wish them worse ?)
May they ne'er the rapture prove
Of the smile from lips we love !

War

War too has sullied Nature's charms,
For gold provokes the world to arms!
And oh! the worst of all its art,
I feel it breaks the lover's heart!

ODE XXX.

'Twas in an airy dream of night,
I fancied that I wing'd my flight.
On pinions fleeter than the wind,
While little Love, whose feet were twin'd
(I know not why) with chains of lead,
Pursued me as I trembling fled;
Pursued—and could I e'er have thought?—
Swift as the moment I was caught!
What does the wanton Fancy mean
By such a strange, illusive scene?

Barnes imagines from this allegory, that our poet married very late in life. I do not perceive any thing in the ode which seems to allude to matrimony, except it be the lead upon the feet of Cupid; and I must confess that I agree in the opinion of Madame Dacier, in her life of the poet, that he was always too fond of pleasure to marry.

I fear

I fear she whispers to my breast,
That you, my girl, have stol'n my rest;
That though my fancy, for a while,
Has hung on many a woman's smile,
I soon dissolv'd the passing vow,
And ne'er was caught by love till now!

ODE

ODE XXXI.

Arm'd with hyacinthine rod,
(Arms enough for such a god,)
Cupid bade me wing my pace,
And try with him the rapid race.

O'er

The design of this little fiction is to intimate, that much greater pain attends insensibility than can ever result from the tenderest impressions of love. Longepierre has quoted an ancient epigram (I do not know where he found it), which has some similitude to this ode:

Lecto compositus, vix prima silentia noctis
    Carpebam, et somno lumina victa dabam;
Cum me sævus Amor prensum, sursumque capillis
    Excitat, et lacerum pervigilare jubet.
Tu famulus meus, inquit, ames cum mille puellas,
    Solus Io, solus, dure jacere potes?
Exilio et pedibus nudis, tunicaque soluta,
    Omne iter impedio, nullum iter expedio.

Nunc

O'er the wild torrent, rude and deep,
By tangled brake and pendent steep,

Nunc propero, nunc ire piget; rursumque redire
  Pœnitet; et pudor est stare via media.
Ecce tacent voces hominum, strepitusque ferarum,
  Et volucrum cantus, turbaque fida canum.
Solus ego ex cunctis paveo somnumque torumque,
  Et sequor imperium, sæve Cupido, tuum.

Upon my couch I lay, at night profound,
My languid eyes in magic slumber bound,
When Cupid came and snatch'd me from my bed,
And forc'd me many a weary way to tread.
" What! (said the god), shall you, whose vows are known,
" Who love so many nymphs, thus sleep alone?"
I rise and follow; all the night I stray,
Unshelter'd, trembling, doubtful of my way.
Tracing with naked foot the painful track,
Loth to proceed, yet fearful to go back.
Yes, at that hour, when Nature seems interr'd,
Nor warbling birds, nor lowing flocks are heard;
I, I alone, a fugitive from rest,
Passion my guide, and madness in my breast,
Wander the world around, unknowing where,
The slave of love, the victim of despair!

2   With

With weary foot I panting flew,

My brow was chill with drops of dew.

And now my soul, exhausted, dying,

To my lip was faintly flying;

My brow was chill with drops of dew.] I have followed those
who read ταιρεν ιδρως for ωιιρεν υδρος; the former is partly
authorized by the MS. which reads ωιιρεν ιδρως.

And now my soul, exhausted, dying,

To my lip was faintly flying; &c.] In the original, he says,
his heart flew to his nose; but our manner more naturally
transfers it to the lips. Such is the effect that Plato tells us
he felt from a kiss, in a distich, quoted by Aulus Gellius:

Την ψυχην Αγαθωνα φιλων, επι χιιλισιν ισχον.

Ηλθι γαρ η τλημων ως διαβησομενη.

Whene'er thy nectar'd kiss I sip,
    And drink thy breath, in melting twine,
My soul then flutters to my lip,
    Ready to fly and mix with thine.

Aulus Gellius subjoins a paraphrase of this epigram, in
which we find many of those mignardises of expression,
which mark the effemination of the Latin language.

And

And now I thought the spark had fled,
When Cupid hover'd o'er my head,
And fanning light his breezy plume,
Recall'd me from my languid gloom;
Then said, in accents half-reproving,
" Why hast thou been a foe to loving?"

And fanning light his breezy plume,
Recall'd me from my languid gloom;]   " The facility with
which Cupid recovers him, signifies that the sweets of love
make us easily forget any solicitudes which he may occasion."
La Fosse.

ODE XXXII.

STREW me a breathing bed of leaves,
Where lotus with the myrtle weaves;
And while in luxury's dream I sink,
Let me the balm of Bacchus drink!

In

We here have the poet, in his true attributes, reclining upon
myrtles, with Cupid for his cup-bearer. Some interpreters
have ruined the picture by making Ερως the name of his slave.
None but Love should fill the goblet of Anacreon. Sappho
has assigned this office to Venus, in a fragment. Ελθι, Κυπρι,
χρυσιαισιν εν κυλικεσιν αβρως συμμεμιγμενον θαλιαισι νεκταρ
οινοχουσα τουτοισι τοις εταιροις εμοις γε και σοις.

Which may be thus paraphrased:

Hither, Venus! queen of kisses,
This shall be the night of blisses!
This the night, to friendship dear,
Thou shalt be our Hebe here.
Fill the golden brimmer high,
Let it sparkle like thine eye!

In this delicious hour of joy,
Young Love shall be my goblet-boy;
Folding his little golden vest,
With cinctures, round his snowy breast,
Himself shall hover by my side,
And minister the racy tide!
Swift as the wheels that kindling roll,
Our life is hurrying to the goal:
A scanty dust, to feed the wind,
Is all the trace 't will leave behind.

Bid the rosy current gush,
Let it mantle like thy blush!
Venus! hast thou e'er above
Seen a feast so rich in love?
Not a soul that is not mine!
Not a soul that is not thine!

"Compare with this ode (says the German commentator) the beautiful poem in Ramler's Lyr. Blumenlese, lib. iv. p. 296. Amor als Diener."

Why

Why do we shed the rose's bloom
Upon the cold, insensate tomb ?
Can flowery breeze, or odour's breath,
Affect the slumbering chill of death ?
No, no; I ask no balm to steep
With fragrant tears my bed of sleep :
But now, while every pulse is glowing,
Now let me breathe the balsam flowing;
Now let the rose, with blush of fire,
Upon my brow its scent expire ;
And bring the nymph with floating eye,
Oh ! she will teach me how to die !
Yes, Cupid ! ere my soul retire,
To join the blest elysian choir,
With wine, and love, and blisses dear,
I 'll make my own elysium here !

ODE XXXIII.

'T was noon of night, when round the pole
The sullen Bear is seen to roll;
And mortals, wearied with the day,
Are slumbering all their cares away:
An infant, at that dreary hour,
Came weeping to my silent bower,

Monsieur Bernard, the author of l'Art d'aimer, has written
a ballet called "Les Surprises de l'Amour," in which the
subject of the third entrée is Anacreon, and the story of this
ode suggests one of the scenes. Œuvres de Bernard. Anac.
scene 4th.

The German annotator refers us here to an imitation by Uz,
lib. iii. "Amor und sein Bruder," and a poem of Kleist die
Heilung. La Fontaine has translated, or rather imitated, this
ode.

5   And

And wak'd me with a piteous prayer,

To save him from the midnight air !

" And who art thou," I waking cry,

" That bid'st my blissful visions fly ?"

" O gentle sire !" the infant said,

" In pity take me to thy shed ;

" Nor fear deceit : a lonely child

" I wander o'er the gloomy wild.

" Chill drops the rain, and not a ray

" Illumes the drear and misty way !"

I hear the baby's tale of woe ;

I hear the bitter night-winds blow ;

And sighing for his piteous fate,

I trimm'd my lamp and op'd the gate.

" And who art thou," I waking cry,

" That bid'st my blissful visions fly ?"] Anacreon appears to
have been a voluptuary even in dreaming, by the lively regret
which he expresses at being disturbed from his visionary en-
joyments. See the odes x. and xxxvii.

'T was

'T was Love! the little wandering sprite,
His pinion sparkled through the night!
I knew him by his bow and dart;
I knew him by my fluttering heart!
I take him in, and fondly raise
The dying embers' cheering blaze;
Press from his dank and clinging hair
The crystals of the freezing air,
And in my hand and bosom hold
His little fingers thrilling cold.
And now the embers' genial ray
Had warm'd his anxious fears away;
" I pray thee," said the wanton child,
(My bosom trembled as he smil'd,)
" I pray thee let me try my bow,
" For through the rain I 've wander'd so, .

'T was Love! the little wandering sprite, &c.] See the beautiful description of Cupid, by Moschus, in his first idyll.

" That

" That much I fear, the ceaseless shower
" Has injur'd its elastic power."
The fatal bow the urchin drew;
Swift from the string the arrow flew;
Oh! swift it flew as glancing flame,
And to my very soul it came!
" Fare thee well," I heard him say,
As laughing wild he wing'd away;
" Fare thee well, for now I know
" The rain has not relax'd my bow;
" It still can send a madd'ning dart,
" As thou shalt own with all thy heart!"

ODE

ODE XXXIV.

Oн thou, of all creation blest,
Sweet insect! that delight'st to rest
Upon the wild wood's leafy tops,
To drink the dew that morning drops,

And

Father Rapin, in a Latin ode addressed to the grasshopper,
has preserved some of the thoughts of our author:

O quæ virenti graminis in toro,
Cicada, blande sidis, et herbidos
　　Saltus oberras, otiosos
　　Ingeniosa ciere cantus.
Seu forte adultis floribus incubas,
Cœli caducis ebria fletibus, &c.

Oh thou, that on the grassy bed
Which Nature's vernal hand has spread,
Reclinest soft, and tun'st thy song,
The dewy herbs and leaves among!

Whether

And chirp thy song with such a glee,

That happiest kings may envy thee!

Whatever decks the velvet field,

Whate'er the circling seasons yield,

Whatever buds, whatever blows,

For thee it buds, for thee it grows.

Nor yet art thou the peasant's fear,

To him thy friendly notes are dear;

Whether thou ly'st on springing flowers,
Drunk with the balmy morning-showers,
Or, &c.

See what Licetus says about grasshoppers, cap. 93 and 185.

And chirp thy song with such a glee, &c.] " Some authors
have affirmed (says Madame Dacier), that it is only male
grasshoppers which sing, and that the females are silent; and
on this circumstance is founded a bon-mot of Xenarchus, the
comic poet, who says ειτ' εισιν δι τιττιγις αχ ιυδαιμονις, ιν ταις
γυναιξιν αδ' ότι αν φωναι ισι; ' are not the grasshoppers happy
in having dumb wives'?" This note is originally Henry
Stephen's; but I chose rather to make Madame Dacier my
authority for it.

For

For thou art mild as matin dew,

And still, when summer's flowery hue

Begins to paint the bloomy plain,

We hear thy sweet, prophetic strain;

Thy sweet, prophetic strain we hear,

And bless the notes and thee revere!

The Muses love thy shrilly tone;

Apollo calls thee all his own;

'T was he who gave that voice to thee,

'T is he who tunes thy minstrelsy.

The Muses love thy shrilly tone; &c.] Phile, de Animal. Proprietat. calls this insect Μουσις φιλος, the darling of the Muses, and Μουων ορνιν, the bird of the Muses; and we find Plato compared for his eloquence to the grasshopper, in the following punning lines of Timon, preserved by Diogenes Laertius:

Των παντων δ' ηγειτο πλατυτατος, αλλ' αγορητης
Ηδυπνης τεττιξιν ισογραφος, οιθ' εκαδημυ
Δενθρεα εφιζομενοι οπα λειριοισσαν ιεισι.

This last line is borrowed from Homer's Iliad, γ. where there occurs the very same simile.

Unworn

Unworn by age's dim decline,

The fadeless blooms of youth are thine.

Melodious insect! child of earth!

In wisdom mirthful, wise in mirth;

Exempt from every weak decay,

That withers vulgar frames away;

With not a drop of blood to stain

The current of thy purer vein;

So blest an age is pass'd by thee,

Thou seem'st—a little deity!

Melodious insect! child of earth!] Longepierre has quoted the two first lines of an epigram of Antipater, from the first book of the Anthologia, where he prefers the grasshopper to the swan :

> Αρμει τεττιγας μαθυσαι δροσος, αλλα πιοντες
> Αιιδειν κυκνων ιισι γεγωνοτεροι.

  In dew, that drops from morning's wings,
    The gay Cicada sipping floats;
  And drunk with dew his matin sings
    Sweeter than any cygnet's notes.

ODE

ODE XXXV.

CUPID once upon a bed
Of roses laid his weary head;
Luckless urchin, not to see
Within the leaves a slumbering bee!.

The

Theocritus has imitated this beautiful ode in his nineteenth idyll, but is very inferior, I think, to his original, in delicacy of point and naïveté of expression. Spenser, in one of his smaller compositions, has sported more diffusely on the same subject. The poem to which I allude, begins thus.

Upon a day, as Love lay sweetly slumbering
All in his mother's lap;
A gentle bee, with his loud trumpet murmuring,
About him flew by hap, &c. &c.

In Almeloveen's collection of epigrams, there is one by Luxorius, correspondent somewhat with the turn of Anacreon, where Love complains to his mother of being wounded by a rose.

The

The bee awak'd—with anger wild
The bee awak'd, and stung the child.
Loud and piteous are his cries;
To Venus quick he runs, he flies!

" Oh

The ode before us is the very flower of simplicity. The infantine complainings of the little god, and the natural and impressive reflections which they draw from Venus, are beauties of inimitable grace. I hope I shall be pardoned for introducing another Greek Anacreontic of Monsieur Menage, not for its similitude to the subject of this ode, but for some faint traces of this natural simplicity, which it appears to me to have preserved:

Ερως ποτ' εν χορειαις
Των παρθενων αυτου
Την μοι φιλην Κοριτταν
'Ως ειδεν, ὡς προς αυτην
Προσεδραμε· τραχηλω
Διδυμας τε χειρας απτων
Φιλει με, μητερ, ειπε.
Καλυμενη Κοριττα,
Μητηρ, ερυθριαξει,
'Ως παρθενος μεν ισα·
Κ' αυτος δε δυσχεραινων,
'Ως ομμασι πλανηθεις,

Ερως

"Oh mother!—I am wounded through—
"I die with pain—in sooth I do!
"Stung by some little angry thing,
"Some serpent on a tiny wing—

                                    "A bee

Ερως ερυθριαζει.
Εγω δι ὁι παρατας,
Μη δυσχιραινι, φημι.
Κυπριν τι και Κορινναν
Διαγνωσαι ακ ιχυσι
Και ὁι βλεποντις οξυ.

As dancing o'er the enamell'd plain,
The flowret of the virgin train,
My soul's Corinna lightly play'd,
Young Cupid saw the graceful maid;
He saw, and in a moment flew,
And round her neck his arms he threw;
And said, with smiles of infant joy,
"Oh! kiss me, mother, kiss thy boy!"
Unconscious of a mother's name,
The modest virgin blush'd with shame!
And angry Cupid, scarce believing
That vision could be so deceiving,
Thus to mistake his Cyprian dame,
The little infant blush'd with shame.

                                    "Be

" A bee it was—for once, I know
" I heard a rustic call it so."
Thus he spoke, and she the while
Heard him with a soothing smile;
Then said, " My infant, if so much
" Thou feel the little wild-bee's touch,
" How must the heart, ah Cupid ! be,
" The hapless heart that 's stung by thee !"

" Be not asham'd, my boy," I cried,
For I was lingering by his side ;
" Corinna and thy lovely mother,
" Believe me, are so like each other,
" That clearest eyes are oft betray'd,
" And take thy Venus for the maid."

Zitto, in his Cappriciosi Pensieri, has translated this ode of Anacreon.

THE END OF THE FIRST VOLUME.

S. GOSNELL, Printer,
Little Queen Street, Holborn.